Praise for *The Dog Who Took Me Up a Mountain*

"Cats may enjoy nine lives, but in Rick Crandall's *The Dog Who Took Me Up a Mountain* we learn how a pint-sized Australian terrier named Emme opened up a new, richly rewarding second life for a man who thought he had it all until his little four-legged giant showed him how to *really* live."

—**Doug McIntyre**, *Los Angeles Daily News/ Orange County Register*

"An amazing journey. Congratulations. Your feat dwarfs others. Your book will be a major success, and it will inspire many into outdoor health, which is a mantra in Colorado."

—**John Hickenlooper**, former Colorado governor

"I enjoyed reading about Rick's adventures in the mountains with his best friend Emme. You should know that I love dogs. Not so crazy about men. But you don't have to love dogs or men to love this book and how it speaks to all of us."

—**Richard Kind**, actor

"I am hugely impressed by your ascents of the fourteeners and your approach to the book—never too late to find a new passion in life."

—**Sir Chris Bonington**, legendary mountaineer, author, lecturer, and still climbing in his 80s

To my wife, Pamela, whose passion for animals made Emme possible and who took many of the photos to help this great story.

THE DOG WHO TOOK ME UP A MOUNTAIN

HOW EMME
THE AUSTRALIAN TERRIER
CHANGED MY LIFE
WHEN I NEEDED IT MOST

RICK CRANDALL
AND JOSEPH COSGRIFF

To Jeff

Rick Crandall

Health Communications, Inc.
Deerfield Beach, Florida

www.hcibooks.com

Library of Congress Cataloging-in-Publication Data
is available through the Library of Congress

© 2019 Rick Crandall

ISBN-13: 978–07573–2268–6 (Paperback)
ISBN-10: 07573–2268–9 (Paperback)
ISBN-13: 978–07573–2269–3 (ePub)
ISBN-10: 07573–2269–7 (ePub)

Publisher: Health Communications, Inc.
          1700 NW 2nd Avenue
          Boca Raton, FL 33432-1653

Cover photo © Rick Crandall
Cover and interior design by Lawna Patterson Oldfield

CONTENTS

PREFACE

For as long as I can remember, my life has been filled with surprises. Not that I'm complaining; although the paths I followed have not been the ones I expected to take, the outcomes have been better than anything I could have hoped for.

I am honored that you have taken time from the demands of your life to open the covers of this book. What I hope to be able to share with you are the unexpected life lessons I experienced in my later-in-life pursuit of an unconventional passion—mountain climbing. I found this passion as part of a relationship I developed with my unlikely best friend, an Australian terrier named Emme (pronounced "emmy").

In ways I'll describe throughout the book, Emme was responsible for my starting to hike in the hills around Aspen, Colorado. An occasional activity became a serious hobby, then blossomed into a full-blown mission. Before long, I would go on to climb every mountain over 14,000 feet in the Rocky Mountains—all fifty-eight of them. Mountain climbers call these "fourteeners," and I didn't climb my first one until I was sixty-four.

What is a person to do for the final twenty or thirty years of life after age sixty? It is a question I have been asking throughout my life, but far more often as I approached sixty. Knowing and watching friends live active lives into their eighties and even their nineties, I am not close to giving up my passion for learning or, better yet, accomplishing things.

I have come away from these experiences in the mountains with a deep conviction. Finding and pursuing a passion—any passion—is as important in one's later years as it is all through life. That newfound passion for me took the form of mountain climbing with my friends and my dog. But the point of this book is to inspire readers to find passion anywhere and in anything that stirs the emotions. My dog taught me to understand that answers and solutions can come from everywhere.

It breaks my heart that Emme was not able to share more of this journey with me. I know that were she with us today, she would want me to continue what the two of us started. For that, I will be forever grateful to her. She both changed my life and extended my life. I am proud to continue down the path on which she set me.

As a scientist and engineer, I had been a deep skeptic of books about inspirational pets, particularly dogs who speak. But that was before I learned how to listen, if only to a tilted head, an angry stare, a wagging tail, or some very human-like action. Emme's enduring spirit is what finally nudged me into the chair to share her story. I hope you enjoy reading about Emme's adventures half as much as I enjoyed being a part of them.

—Rick Crandall,
Aspen, CO

Acknowledgments

I thought I could create this book all by myself. Then, as I got into this project, the first thought that hit my mind was that Emme didn't just arrive out of the blue; it was the genius of my wife Pamela, not only to set as her silent goal to find me a companion for Aspen outdoor activities, but also to select Emme from a lot of choices, to train her, and to deal with her early alpha-female take-charge attitude. Pamela put up with a lot in raising Emme. When I got her for our mountain adventures, Emme's irrepressible personality was all positives. Without Pamela's efforts, however, there would be no Emme and no book. Thank you, Pamela; it is still a mystery how you found and raised such a unique animal, but as a result I had the most fun nine years in my life with Emme as my companion in the mountains.

I wrote stories on each of the major climbs. They weren't really stories; they were picture essays accompanied by some words that relied heavily on the photos. Once I got into this book project, I realized the words needed to be expressive on their own merit without relying on photos. That was more challenging, and thankfully, Tom Juhase introduced me to Joe Cosgriff, an author in his own right, who was willing to help me with the writing. Joe has a great combination of being expressive in his writing and capturing the adventure and the humor in what Emme and I were doing. I had some goals, and this book nails them—thank you, Joe, for putting up with me.

Then there is Doug Grad, my agent. He saw my stories on *rickcrandall.net* and when we met, he said, "I'll take you on, but I see more than one book here. Your first book must be the great collection of stories that define the unique relationship between you and your dog—going for incredible mountain summits despite your age and her small size." And that is what we did. Thank you, Doug.

Christine Belleris, editor at HCI Books, saw our overview of this book and took no time to put HCI on the team. She loves dogs, and, as a native Coloradoan living in exile in Florida, she loves the Rocky Mountains. I had heard that sometimes dealing with a publisher's editor can be a tough experience. Not here. I felt her enthusiasm for this book right from the outset, and all during the creative effort, she edited, she questioned, and she contributed in ways that always made sense and made the book better. Thank you, Christine.

Finally, even before Joe got involved, when I thought it was my job to create the 55,000-plus words—I got help from some great friends who are themselves authors. Dexter Cirillo, Gay Campbell, Judy Hamilton, and Tania Amochaev, plus one of my sons, Clayton—thank you for the countless times you reread the growing manuscript, gave me direct feedback, sometimes right between the eyes, and helped me get the text ready for Joe to make even better.

While each of my hiking/climbing buddies is mentioned in the book, my deep appreciation goes to Shan Stuart, Laura Welch, Rick Peckham, Andy Mishmash, and my son, Brett Crandall, without whom the climbs never would have happened. It has been quite the learning experience as to how many people it takes to make a successful book project. There are many more I have not mentioned by name here, but you know who you are, and you have my heartfelt thanks for your help.

And to the memory of you, Emme—what can I say other than thank you for giving me the greatest gift of finding a new passion later in life.

CHAPTER 1

Let's Get a Dog

Love me when I least deserve it because
that's when I really need it.

—Swedish Proverb

My name is Rick Crandall. In 1966, I graduated from the University of Michigan (#GoBlue) and soon afterward co-founded Comshare, Inc., one of the earliest computer timesharing companies in Ann Arbor, Michigan. These were the prehistoric days of the industry, before advances in solid-state physics that made possible the invention of the microchip in 1972. The internet and the first personal computers were still decades away. I was just twenty-two years old.

But after our talented team defied long odds to keep the company relevant, innovative, and (mostly) profitable for over twenty-five years, I found myself in my mid fifties and burned out mentally, physically, and spiritually. When I took what seemed like a logical next career step—serving on tech company boards and coaching early-stage start-ups—the future felt more uncertain than at any time in my life. While the companies I advised experienced little if any difficulty in transitioning to Y2K, the early days of the year 2000 continued to produce disorder and disruption for me because of the emotional lows and anxieties that were the fallout of a sad and difficult divorce.

Around that same time our only child, my son Brett, graduated from high school and enrolled at NYU, 623 miles to the east in New York City. After our trip to the East Coast the previous year, Brett was so completely won over by Manhattan and the idea of attending a college located in the heart of this bustling metropolis that I could not even convince him to apply to a second or third choice of colleges. This approach was consistent with his successful, lifelong practice of bringing a laser-like focus to achieving his most serious goals. While I might have considered a backup plan and told him so, Brett wouldn't hear of such a thing. And no backups were needed as it turned out: he was accepted by the only school to which he had applied—NYU's Stern Undergraduate College.

The year was also marked by the death of my beloved dad—an accomplished businessman and a decorated World War II veteran who had been wounded in action. But more important than the credentials in his bio, he was a gentle giant who always had my back and made it his role to mediate any problems within our family. Even as he was getting up in years, I had never allowed myself to consider a world without my father in it.

With Brett leaving for NYU and in need of a permanent new home of my own, I began to at least consider a clean break from Michigan. When my doctors informed me that I had an acute case of Seasonal Affective Disorder, officially categorized as a "serious depression" that was related to a lack of sunlight in the winter months—something I'd been feeling more and more over the years but didn't realize—their diagnosis sealed the deal. Besides assigning a name to the health issue, my doctors were vocal in urging me to find a place to live that has significantly more sunny days each year than Ann Arbor. There were many reasons to love Ann Arbor, or I would not have called the town my home for almost forty years. And don't take my word for it—*Forbes* and *CNN Money* were among the publications that regularly included Ann Arbor among the best places to live in the United States. In fact, two lifestyle websites recently gave Ann Arbor its highest honors—*niche .com* as "Best City" (2017) and *Livability.com* as the #1 "Best Place to Live" (2018).

But as much as Ann Arbor fit me like an old pair of Levi's for so many years, the doctors continued to insist that the fifty-seven-year-old version of me needed more sunny days, particularly from October through April. A quick Google search for "cities with most sunlight" and "more sun than Ann Arbor" immediately produced a list of qualifying cities and towns ranging from sea to shining sea. In fact, it included just about *every* city, with the exceptions of Portland, Seattle, Pittsburgh, and several Midwestern cities.

Colorado—especially the Denver and Aspen areas—appeared high on every statistical list of annual sunny hours and average number of sunny days. That said, I don't recall applying my usual due diligence or an exhaustive decision-making process when it came to the choice of the Aspen area as my new home. Our family had taken ski trips out there about once a year, and a catchy tourism slogan had stuck with me over the years—"Aspen: Come for the winter, stay for the summer." As major decisions go, this one was as impulsive as it gets for me.

Sunny, gorgeous, near an airport with major airlines—check, check, check for Aspen. The only issue? Living in Washtenaw County, Michigan, for so long had not prepared me for the sticker shock of Aspen's home prices. The resort town had clearly come a long way in almost 140 years—from its days as a small silver mining community to a stunning, world-famous ski mecca. Two dozen art galleries and an airport filled with private jets should have been a giveaway that Aspen was now both home to, and destination of, the best-heeled among the well-heeled. And the asking prices of homes within Aspen made one wonder if a private jet were not included in the real estate prices I was seeing.

It was amid these major life transitions back in 2000 that I found myself swept off my feet by a woman named Pamela Levy. My consulting business led to considerable travel throughout the United States, serving on boards of several technology companies. It was through my work at one such company where Pamela worked as the executive advisor to the CEO that she and I became acquainted. I was finalizing my divorce as she was exiting a relationship, and so the emails began.

After enough words passed between us to fill a Russian novel, we finally decided to meet in person to pursue this relationship. By all measures, it was an inspired idea both in its imagination and execution. Lucille Ball probably said it best—"It wasn't love at

Pamela and me in the early days of our relationship.

first sight. It took a full five minutes." After a headlong dive into an emotional, whirlwind courtship, Pamela and I were married in August 2000. We were thrilled that Pamela's son, Clayton, and my son, Brett, not only attended the festivities but also ventured out together on an eventful early morning rock climb on our wedding day, which they both survived (more on that later).

A few words about Pamela—at the center of her personality is the heart of an activist warrior always seeking to right injustices so that those who follow will not need to endure them. She is smart, creative, and quick-witted. And in contrast to my rational approach to most situations, Pamela has a more spiritual approach, such as when she prefers to consult with Chinese astrologers.

Having once lived in Aspen for six years, Pamela had the valuable asset of local knowledge when it came to compiling a list of homes that met our criteria. She extended the search to about ten minutes outside Aspen proper, which is how we wound up buying in the funky, rustic town of Woody Creek (population 263). The loft-style house was in fact a converted storage garage that had been maintained by a wealthy car collector. The good news is that there was no need to inspect under the floorboards for used antifreeze; the floor was solid, polished concrete.

Woody Creek is best-known as the hometown of the late gonzo journalist, Hunter S. Thompson (*Fear and Loathing in Las Vegas*), whose home has been transformed into a writers' retreat and a museum. The local version of things is that in 2005, and in rapidly failing health, Mr. Thompson enjoyed a breakfast of fresh fruit and Jell-O splashed with gin and Grand Marnier—and then ended his life. In keeping with his wishes, his ashes were shot from a 100-foot cannon on his property at Owl Farm. Whether it was gazing at the mountain peaks for minutes at a time, acquainting myself with a product called "sunscreen," or engaging in conversations with my new neighbors at the Woody Creek Tavern, I often caught myself silently repeating, *I have a feeling I'm not in Ann Arbor anymore.*

Pamela and I had contrasting styles, but it seemed to work, probably because we understood almost immediately that we both required independence and support in following our individual passions. In this spirit, Pamela introduced a new subject one morning over coffee, six months into our marriage.

"Let's get a dog. I love animals and can't picture my life without them."

The request didn't take me entirely by surprise. From the start, I knew that Pamela was an animal person and that pets would be part of our future. I just didn't want to jump into the constraints of animal ownership and care so early on in our marriage. To be honest, I had stars in my eyes about a life with my new wife—as well as our freedom to both travel extensively and to participate in the outdoor social events that are so popular in the Aspen area. Four years removed from the full-time grind, I now found myself with a manageable schedule of board obligations and a set of advisor roles that often allowed me to contribute by phone and email. If people of a certain age were ranking the advantages of the "senior tour," flexibility of schedule would have to rank number one or close to it. A new dog would entail a rigidity of schedule and limitations to our lifestyle that I was certainly hesitant to embrace.

"How about we not get too tied down just yet? Maybe travel, do what we want whenever we want."

"I've been doing my research, and I even know what dog breed I want to get."

A happy wife equals a happy life, I thought—and repeated six times silently.

"Okay."

There were at least two good reasons for me to instantly agree to our having a dog. One was that Pamela had been lightly floating the idea of a pet monkey. Not only are monkeys *wild animals* that bite when touched, they cost up to $10,000 a year to maintain properly and can also be counted upon to urinate on every inch of a private home to mark their territory. Just in case the subject came up again, I'd saved an entire quote from my internet research: "I am a primatologist. I have dedicated my life to working with primates. There is not a chance I would want one as a pet."

Argument number two for a dog is that it would also represent a marked upgrade from Pamela's most recent pet, a Savannah serval cat named Simba that she owned during the months that we were dating. And for good measure, hers was an F1 generation cat, which meant it was a breeding step (or a step and a half) removed from the African serval cat, which also qualifies as a wild animal.

In upholding the traditions of its ancestors, Pamela's Savannah cat preferred to hunt in the middle of the night, usually in our bedroom. She prowled as though at any moment she intended to pounce onto one of us or something we didn't see. Simba's résumé included a seven-foot vertical leap, as well as its species' habit of marking its favorite territories, one of which turned out to be my chest. One night, she leaped from the floor from the far side of a king bed, landed on my chest, and stared into my face while she proceeded to pee while pinning me down. The overnight hours were like sleeping in a zoo, only we were *inside* the cage. You can understand why I eventually trained myself to snooze with at least one eye open.

Pamela reluctantly donated the cat to an animal sanctuary that was equipped to handle wild and semi-wild animals. She had gone to visit her son, Clayton, in Florida, transporting the female cat in an underseat animal carrier. But when it came time to place Simba back in the carrier for the return trip, the cat was having none of it. Upon hearing the hissing and seeing the fangs, Clayton appreciated the gravity of the situation. A motorcycle enthusiast, Clayton thought he could accomplish getting her back in the carrier, but only after donning protective gear. On went the leather jacket, pants, and gloves, as well as his helmet with visor, to protect himself from Simba's claws and teeth. Envisioning a similar scene at the TSA departure checkpoint, Pamela and Clayton arrived at the practical decision to find the cat a suitable home—coincidentally, not far from the airport.

Upon Pamela's arrival back in Colorado, we had officially become pet "empty-nesters." So, after I fended off the idea of a pet monkey and somehow survived the serval cat's hunting season, the suggestion (okay, it was a strong request) over morning coffee that we add a dog to our family sounded reasonable indeed. Just not a wild animal.

It was around this same time that the full impact of the collapse of the so-called "tech bubble" and its resulting loss of $5 trillion of stock value began to hit home. As a lifelong tech guy with full confidence in the industry that had defined my business career, I ignored the obvious signs and wound up riding the elevator to the basement. The conventional wisdom was that there would be a 10 to 15 percent correction of stock prices that we now see were based more on the vague promise of "technology" rather than on the fundamentals of strong cash flow and profitability. With the benefit of twenty-twenty hindsight, I should have gotten out far sooner than I did. But it was the opinion of many industry colleagues, probably also analyzing with their hearts, that the large drops in tech stocks would correct and adjust upward. In the end, it was a mess. You knew it was bad when the *Pets.com* sock puppet—star of the 2000 Super Bowl—was liquidated along with his company less than a year after he starred in a series of coast-to-coast commercials that had cost the company millions. It was a questionable decision, the business press suggested in the postmortems, to sell so many twenty-pound bags of dog and cat food at prices below the company's internal costs.

By the time the dust had settled, there had been a dramatic reduction in the nest egg that was supposed to sustain Pamela and me through our retirement years. Combined with the financial terms of my divorce a year and a half earlier, "Mr. Market" (as a friend referred to market forces of all kinds) had taught me long division in a manner that was harsh and unsparing. The idea of starting over in my late fifties was daunting, particularly in 2001, when youth seemed to be the valued credential of choice in the tech world. This was underscored by a sign at the main entrance to the 2001 Comdex computer show at the Las Vegas Convention Center—*"No admittance to minors under eighteen years of age unless you are the CEO of a software company."* But it didn't take a sign at a convention hall for me to read the writing on the wall—for the first time in my life I suddenly felt old.

This was also a first for me in experiencing a business-related failure on this level. In my mind, I had made the wrong choices for all the right reasons. The technology industry had provided me with everything I had on Earth, and I had tremendous faith in the underlying power of how it would continue to transform the world (and it has). What I had not considered was that with so many tech stocks in my portfolio—because that was often the primary form of compensation for board positions and for consulting with start-ups—I had left myself vulnerable to a bubble burst that could take down the entire sector—good and bad stocks alike.

My life and career up to that point had been defined by a decisive and confident attitude, always driving things forward, even when roads led to the unknown. But something was different this time. Rebuilding our financial stability felt like a tall mountain to climb, especially for someone whose opportunities were shrinking and whose AARP membership was out of place in a young person's tech world.

As these realities took hold and an overall melancholy set in, I'll be the first to admit that my behavior suffered. It is an understatement that I was not always the most pleasant person to be sharing a home and a bed, and this situation was not lost on Pamela. It had to be a new wife's nightmare—the older but (until now) vibrant new husband hitting a self-made wall and being thrown off-balance by a blue funk of depression. This challenge in our marriage revealed that Pamela was a disciple of the Law of Attraction—that what you think about and focus on are what you will attract into your life.

"It will all work out; new things will come your way," she would often say. To her credit, Pamela also walked the talk, continuing to give me plenty of room and making it clear she believed that only I could "fix" me.

My attitude was poles apart from Pamela's at that time. My approach to life was more along the lines of "Things don't happen just by thinking about them; I need to *make* them happen."

Slowly, I began to try to figure out what I would need to do to pull myself out of this spiral. It would involve (1) snapping out of this strange and unfamiliar state of depression, and (2) stabilizing and rebuilding our financial situation. Yogi Berra famously said, "When you come to a fork in the road, take it." I had unquestionably arrived at a fork in the road in April 2001, and it was one ablaze with red lights and stop signs that froze me in my tracks. Maybe the answer here was to simply follow Mr. Berra's sage advice—not to overanalyze which was the better road leading out of this unexpected predicament, but to "take it."

Meanwhile, the idea of getting a dog appealed to me more each day, and not just because a dog spared me from the alternatives— the biting and scratching of a wild monkey or the nocturnal bedroom hunting of a Savannah cat. Things had gotten quiet around the house for any number of reasons, and a dog might keep me from obsessing on the new normal of our finances, as well as providing Pamela and me with a new family member we could talk about and play with together.

During my days on the dark side, Pamela had continued to plow ahead with research on a breed that would be the best for us. She said she began by casting a wide net, with no hard-and-fast requirements other than friendly, intelligent, and compatible with modest hiking in conditions like Aspen's.

Then one morning Pamela broke the news that she had arrived at a final decision—that we would be adding an Australian terrier to our household. It turned out she had recently happened upon an Aussie terrier in a pet shop while traveling, looked up the breed online, and became intrigued. Conveniently, that month's issue of *Terrier Type* magazine featured the Australian terrier from cover to cover, so she sent for it and studied it carefully. It was after this round of due diligence that she initiated discussions with a handful of quality breeders from around the country. To ensure that she would be selecting from among the best-looking Australian terrier puppies, she added the qualification that our future housemate be "show quality." This added condition, she insisted, had zero to do with ever hitting the *Best in Show* circuit and everything to do with increasing our chances of receiving a truly beautiful and healthy dog.

It was obvious Pamela had done her homework, as she enthusiastically spelled out the qualities of the Australian terrier for about fifteen minutes. One description of the breed to which she repeatedly circled back was "Big dogs in small bodies." But for good measure, she quickly mentioned even more positives:

- Not yappy;
- No shedding;
- Fits in carriers under the seat of airplanes; and
- Enjoys outdoor activities.

As for my take on Australian terriers, I hadn't even known the breed existed. Regarding the characteristics she said they possessed, except for fitting under the airplane seat, she just as well could have been talking about me (especially "not yappy"). I figured she had put so much thought and research into the selection that I was happy to go along with whatever she had decided. Remember—*"A happy wife equals..."*

An Australian terrier it would be.

With my head down and immersed in figuring out the new normal of our finances, I cannot say for sure how long it took for

Pamela to narrow her list of candidates to one specific puppy. I do know she felt a certain level of stress in making a final choice based largely on a dog's lineage and photos viewed on a computer screen. Ideally, she wished she had visited the breeder's home and spent time with at least one of the puppy's parents to get a sense of the temperament that would be passed along. She had read of due diligence for puppies coming close to the elaborate interview processes undertaken by the elite preschools in New York City.

Sure, the breeder was reputable, and the puppy on the top of Pamela's list had descended from a long line of champions. But what is a "champion"? At least to this untrained reader, dog breeders' literature invoked more categories of champions than in a fifth-graders' soccer tournament.

Make no mistake—Pamela had been a quick study in the intricate world of the various breeds of dogs and, later, in differentiating among breeders. But she also knew what she didn't know, which was that plunging into online websites about dogs for a few months didn't mean she was qualified to hang a shingle as a dog expert. Fortunately, Pamela's approach to this and to many life decisions has been to trust the process—and then take a leap of faith.

As the day neared when Pamela would drive to Denver International Airport to pick up our new dog, I must confess that my thoughts harkened back to a kooky canine from my adult life, a standard poodle that was inclined to bite humans—mostly unsuspecting joggers as they trotted past our home. Unbeknownst to me, my ex-wife had reached out for professional help (for the poodle), which led to my coming home from work one day to find my wife and a dog psychologist sitting on the floor with the patient.

"We're communicating with the dog at its level," were her first words as I came upon the scene, as though I might have suspected otherwise. It was far above my pay grade to even consider questioning the doctor's methods. I can say that after three sessions of psychological intervention at rates I can only describe as "considerable," it pained me when the poodle showed off his behavioral training by answering the doorbell with us and immediately biting the rabbi's wife.

It wasn't long after the hit on the rabbi's wife that all three of us—my ex-wife, me, and the doggie shrink—waved the white flag of surrender, with the shrink explaining away the standard poodle's temperament with a shrug and scientific explanation "luck of the draw." And while I expected something more complex based on the gentleman's fee schedule, I was inclined to agree. Even within the same breed, dogs always seemed to be different from one another. What if we came up short on the "luck of the draw"? Of course, there had been my childhood dog, Jiggs, which also represented the luck of the draw—the other side. Our family's time with Jiggs was like winning the lottery. These things can go either way.

Fortunately, Pamela is a pet person, and I had complete confidence that she would bring home a third member of our family who would be special and unique. As I look back nearly twenty years later, there was no possible way I could have anticipated just how special and unique our third family member would turn out to be.

CHAPTER 2

Pint-Sized Pup, Giant Personality

We'd begun to long for the pitter-patter
of little feet, so we bought a dog.
It's cheaper, and you get more feet.

—Rita Rudner

Puppy Emme upon arrival.

Perhaps because it was one of the most magical days of my life, I recall the details so vividly. The date was Thursday, April 5, 2001, and the normally painted-blue Rocky Mountain sky had taken a holiday, replaced by charcoal gray and an uncharacteristic full day of dreary, soaking rain. But unlike southeastern Michigan, where this would be a repeat scenario, Woody Creek has years of highly favorable *average sunlight* data in its favor. It's easier to deal with the gloom when you can expect a sunny day right around the corner. Besides which, my spirits were buoyed by the anticipation of the furry new addition to our family. A little drizzle was just a minor inconvenience.

Pamela and I had circled "April 5" on the calendar for weeks, once it was confirmed that a third member would officially be joining our family on that day. But as it turned out, I was hit with two important business meetings and a board call that overlapped with the pickup time, which left Pamela to serve solo as the official welcoming committee. Always a trooper, she embarked in the early morning darkness on the four-hour drive to Denver International Airport. Once there she had arrangements to meet a friend of the Oregon breeder, who would hand over our permanent houseguest.

Fortunately, the last of the day's meetings finished early, allowing me to head home in midafternoon with considerably more anticipation than I had expected to feel. When I walked into the house, I was greeted by the sight of my wife, sitting on the living room floor and wearing a smile that just beamed. Jumping around next to her was one of the smallest dogs I had ever seen—there were pastrami sandwiches at Katz's Deli that were larger and weighed more than this puppy. As befitting a classic version of a blue-and-tan Aussie, she had a brilliant black coat with scattered single gray hairs, which gave the effect of "bluing." Thus, the 1880s name when the dog was first shown—"Broken-coated terrier of blackish blue sheen." No high-resolution photographs from a breeder could do justice to the genuine article that sat before us on the floor at this moment.

Once I entered the room, greeted Pamela, and sat down to join in the party, all playing immediately ceased. Our new family member immediately made me the focus of her attention, making eye contact with her shining black eyes and appearing to listen for signs of trouble with her erect, V-shaped ears. Sitting perfectly still, the puppy continued to stare at me with her head cocked, as though trying to figure out whether I had the credentials to be there. Then she turned her head and shot a pained look at Pamela, as if to say: *What is this guy doing here? We had a good thing going.*

Pamela had decided prior to the puppy's homecoming to name our new pup "Emme" (pronounced EM-me, as in the Emmy Awards). I am still not sure if she chose the name after Emma of Normandy (who married brothers and became Queen of England *twice*), the German root of "irm" and "erm" which means "strength," or because she simply found it to be unique among dog names and in its spelling. Emme was registered with the American Kennel Club as Lucky Lady Emme, a name chosen by Pamela because she figured Emme had lucked out in drawing loving housemates, as well as a place to live that would offer her no limit on outdoor activities.

But we immediately recognized about midway through her first day that Emme's reaction to me was not grounded in fear—she just needed to stare at me for a while and get a feel for where she would be living. Within a short time, she began to display the personality traits I can best describe as a Rottweiler with ADD (with apologies to Rottweilers and those who suffer from Attention Deficit Disorder). Stature and size notwithstanding, Emme considered herself to be an "alpha" female, which, along with my darling wife, added up to two alpha females under the one roof. I decided to look at the bright side; it could be worse. I would be outnumbered by three-to-one had Simba the nocturnal-hunting Savannah cat not relocated to Florida.

Upon diving into online research about the standards of the breed of our new leader, I became convinced that in Emme, we were sharing our home with a slightly exaggerated version of a so-called "normal" Australian terrier. "Jumps into life with an attitude"—absolutely and then some. "Has the confidence of a larger dog"—she carries herself as though she were multiple times her size. "Wants to be a pack leader, even among people"—let's just say that I wouldn't have been surprised had she found a way to change all our computer passwords. And anytime Pamela and I left our home, there was never any question that Emme would be coming along for the ride. She would read signs we were going somewhere—putting on a coat or shoes, Pamela picking up her purse—and Emme would instantly race to the front door, tail wagging, and head swinging from looking at us and looking at the door. You couldn't miss the communication. And try to open the door and keep her in? No way!

After about a week of assessing her domestic situation, our newest family member went about appointing herself as the ranking officer of our household. I am not kidding. How did I conclude that in her mind she "owned" the house? Okay, she didn't pay the mortgage, but she did make rounds every evening as a security guard would, meticulously checking every room. She would then stop at each window and door to look for or sniff out what she deemed to be suspicious animal activities. And when she detected a fox, chipmunk, or deer, she would notify her staff—Pamela and me—with a series of high-pitched barks, followed by angry growling in the lower register. It was a series of sounds markedly different than what she'd established as the "Visitors at the door" bark.

As cute as all of this sounds, Emme was not an easy dog to raise to adulthood, which for the Australian terrier is about two years. And the brunt of Emme's early training fell to Pamela because I was often away on business trips and because she insisted on taking this journey with Emme. In those early days when I would get home from my travels, rather than greet me with a wagging tail as most dogs would, Emme would look at me, seem to shake her head, and then walk away in disgust. She acted almost resentful that I had been away for even a day or two. Only after freezing me out for fifteen or twenty minutes would she return to where I was, eventually warming up and wanting to play. But she was rarely up for playing when I got home from a trip until I spent some time in the penalty box. Or as hockey announcers accurately refer to it—*le Château Bow-Wow*.

The scouting report on Australian terriers is straightforward about their thriving on exercise, especially those bred for hunting and herding. Aware of this from Emme's early days, Pamela began taking our puppy for walks along the Roaring Fork River (nationally renowned for trout fishing), a trail we could join a few miles from our home. Wanting to show me the route of their walks and a chance to see our now four-month-old Emme in action, she suggested one Saturday that all three of us drive over to the trail that starts at Jaffe Park. Emme assumed a position on the center console between the two front seats of our Toyota 4Runner, reminiscent of our first president's pose in Leutze's painting, *Washington Crossing the Delaware*. Meanwhile, Pamela and I were so caught up in a conversation that we drove past the turnoff to the hiking spot. But while we missed the exit, Emme most assuredly did not. *Noooooooo*, she seemed to say, as she began to bark for all she was worth. Neither Pamela nor I spoke "Aussie terrier," but there was no mistaking what Emme seemed to be saying, which was something close to *What's going on here? You just missed the turn for* my *hike. Make a legal U-turn.*

As the barking continued, Pamela and I looked at one another in utter amazement. Did our new puppy's barking binge happen to coincide with the precise moment we drove past the regular hiking exit? Or had our dog somehow memorized the roads that took her to the river, and was she letting us know in no uncertain terms that we had screwed up the directions? That question was answered in seconds when we made a U-turn, a change in direction that immediately brought Emme's barking to an end.

Not trusting us after the missed exit, Emme insisted upon standing on the middle console for every ride from that day forward. It was roughly an 8" × 12" area that allowed no movement to the side or forward for her four feet, so she mastered the skill of bending into turns to retain her balance. The roads in the Woody Creek/Aspen area provide plenty of curves, but Emme was a quick study in how to stabilize herself by leaning forward when I accelerated and leaning back when I needed to brake.

Pamela and I often wondered why Emme chose this vantage point for car rides, but it seemed to make sense as we grew accustomed to her ritual of standing on the console. We figured it was consistent with her breed to want to see the road, rather than nap in the back seat. And she also took pride in how quickly she had taught herself to adjust on the fly to the hairpin turns I frequently took with too much speed. *Not bad, eh?* she seemed to say, as she calmly looked up at me after console surfing through one hairpin turn. And let's not forget—Emme also needed to be in the cat bird's seat because she was not about to allow her human transportation employees to miss her hiking exit ever again.

On that day's short hike and on many of the early ones with her along the Roaring Fork River, Emme would confidently march along ahead of us off-leash, always sniffing to the right, left, and center. Her rules of engagement from the start when encountering other dogs would be to stop, exchange sniffs with her canine brother or sister, unmistakably assert herself as the alpha, and then move on. She had a gruff, short growl combined with getting right into other dogs' faces that at times looked like an attempt at an intimidating stare. Somehow, no other dog wanted to mess with her and, if another dog attempted a challenge, she would literally start sounding vicious to the point that the other dog would roll over on their back and submit. Emme had more important business. It wasn't long before she expanded her explorations right down to the edge of the rapidly flowing river. This made Pamela more nervous than it did me, although I did see her point. While fearless in her heart and flawless in her footwork, our puppy was still only a few months old and weighed only six pounds.

Perhaps Emme felt so emotionally connected with hiking

because she was so naturally skilled at negotiating the outdoors from the first moment she set foot on a trail. For example, when a path is covered in mud, 90 percent of dogs I have seen over the years would walk through the mud and make a general mess of things, at least for the first few trips. But not Emme. From the first time I saw her on the river trail, she immediately side-stepped any mud by walking on the edge of the trail or by landing her steps on rocks that protruded from the mud, an approach Pamela confirmed she had taken from their very first walk together. Somehow, Emme had the brainpower to evaluate a situation she had never seen, weigh possible outcomes, and then figure it out—all before she was ten weeks old. Pamela and I marveled at her innate ingenuity, as well as her sense of accomplishment in the occasional but unmistakable side glance that seemed to say, *What did you expect? Hikes are what I do.*

Without my consciously realizing it, Emme had begun to provide a happy distraction away from the financial predicament that had demanded my full attention and succeeded in darkening my mood just a few months earlier. The bank balances had not appreciably improved, but there was now a third family member in the mix, and I could not help but become more involved with our dog's life. Emme and I didn't discuss politics, world history, or craft beers, but I did discover that we had a possible Major League prospect living with us—had MLB had the foresight to organize a league for dogs.

I know what you're saying—every dog out there can catch a ball. Or at least catch one of five, which is the video the owner will choose to post on YouTube. But after sixty years spent analyzing the ball-catching abilities of dogs, I can tell you that at least 75 percent (or more) make the error of jumping for the ball as soon as the human thrower cocks his or her arm. The miscalculation leads to the dog descending from the peak point in the jump at the precise moment he or she should be at the highest point and catching the ball. This example of bad timing will frequently result in a "miss"—an awkward moment for the dog, the dog's owner, and often, for the underwhelmed audience that has been assembled to "Watch this."

It takes a perceptive and resourceful dog to figure out early that catching occurs more often when timing the jump based on the ball's flight path, which can only be accomplished by waiting for the ball-thrower to release the ball. It took Emme exactly two repetitions to crack the code, after which she became as graceful and athletic as Willie Mays as she soared into the air and snatched every catchable fly ball that came her way. It was a game we could play for easily an hour or more in those days, with Emme taking the occasional timeout to shake her head and puff her chest in triumph after an especially difficult catch. When the fun ended before Emme believed it should, she threw the ball back to us to get things going again. She learned to pick up the ball in her mouth, swing her head to one side, and open her mouth to let go of the ball. I probably don't need to tell you that her aim became reliably dead-on with practice, with a wet and soggy ball regularly winding up squarely in my lap or bouncing off my chest. She later taught herself to throw the ball high into the air and easily catch it herself, a trick that sounds easy enough but is up there with any of David Letterman's "Stupid Pet Tricks" segments.

Yes, I realize I should have recorded all of this for posterity on YouTube. But in the absence of video evidence, I can only say—as with so many things Emme did and "said"—you should have been there.

Just as Pamela hoped (and planned) would take place, Emme was fast beginning to win my heart. My feelings for our new puppy transported me back to the happy memories of my childhood on Long Island and my family's beloved dog that I had mentioned earlier, a Boston terrier named Jiggs. In our trips with Dad to McCluskey's Steakhouse in Bellmore to pick up takeout for dinner, one of the regulars at the bar would always bring along his Boston terrier Jiggs as his companion. We thought that Jiggs was cool, especially how he occupied his own barstool. We wanted a Jiggs.

Against any rational odds, my parents agreed.

The following Saturday, we found ourselves at the home of a breeder my dad had found in the Yellow Pages (the Google of its day), in the presence of a five-puppy litter of, yes, Boston terriers. Soon after we got a look at them, one of the puppies marched directly toward me, separating himself from the group. And with that, it was all over. On the ride home, we spit-balled a few names around but in the end decided not to overthink things. We named him Jiggs.

Our parents made clear that Jiggs was a gift for all the kids—sister Bev, my brother Jerry, and me. It was a great experience for me, as I assumed much of the responsibility for feeding and generally taking care of him. (Not having yet been born when Jiggs arrived, brother Wayne received an exemption from these duties.) The eldest by five years, I was the most responsible but I also chose to do this and enjoyed the job. The three of us spent all our spare time playing with Jiggs in our backyard in Merrick, Long Island. It was a terrific place to grow up, surrounded as we were by upbeat and mostly friendly neighbors in a town made up mainly of split-level homes and yards that were separated by split-rail fences and bushes.

My brother Jerry with our childhood dog, Jiggs.

When I describe the neighbors as "mostly friendly," one can conclude there was at least one sourpuss who lived nearby. In my thirteen-year-old's mind, he was not just a minor annoyance but a nightmare. We'll just call him "Mr. Angry," and he happened to live directly next door to us. He was one of those neighbors whose public face ranged from annoyed to irritable, doubly so when a kid would get careless and make eye contact with him.

Anyone who has ever lived in the suburbs knows that there are two kinds of neighbors—(a) the ones who will happily return the balls/Frisbees/model airplanes that make their way into their yards in the natural course of kid-based activities, and (b) the ones who don't. Mr. Angry had firmly established his membership in camp (b), often making an outsized gesture of lifting his

garbage-can lid and, with a dramatic flourish, dispatching the tres-
passing object to the gods of municipal sanitation.

A useful fact about Mr. Angry—he was over-the-top obses-
sive about his lawn. There was a rumor among the surrounding
neighbors that he was seen on his knees using scissors following
a standard lawn-mowing to ensure that all the blades of grass were
the same length, although, to be sure, no one had witnessed this
unusual spectacle firsthand.

In the interest of full disclosure, the reader should also be
aware that I had the strong sense that Mr. Angry suspected me
in the much-discussed raw eggs-and-firecrackers-in-the-mailbox
incident that took place back on April Fool's Day. (For the record,
I will neither confirm nor deny involvement.) I can confidently
state that the firecrackers in question were the smallest and least
powerful ones available in the United States at that time and were
meant to create mayhem rather than damage or injury.

It was in this context that we realized that we had an asset on
our side that would bring balance in the war against losing our stuff
over the fence—Jiggs! On his own, he learned to crawl covertly
along the bushes that lined the fence until he was the shortest
distance from what he needed to retrieve. Because Mr. Angry had
not buried his fence, Jiggs could then slip under the fence and run
toward the object, grab it while executing a 180-degree turn in a
blur, and shoot back under the fence. It all seemed to take less than
a second, although it never occurred to us to grab a stopwatch and
make it official. When tallied up over Jiggs's career, these mad
dashes probably numbered over a hundred, with Jiggs turning
each one into a black-ops, life-or-death recovery mission at which
he was never caught. Or so we believed.

Then one Saturday morning, I returned home to see Mr. A. at our front door, engaging in a heated conversation with my dad. He alternated between wildly gesturing at his immaculate lawn and pointing at a second location, which looked to be the fence that divided our properties. As much as I wanted to get closer to the exchange than behind a tree two houses away, I thought it best to rely on my father to resolve the situation. At over 6'2" and an ex-military guy, my dad and his calm demeanor appeared to blunt Mr. Angry's early charge. Always favorably comparing my dad to other fathers, I recall hoping the two men would decide to settle the issue on a football field or a basketball court. My dad would have won for sure, given that he enjoyed a seven- or eight-inch height advantage over the tiny tyrant from next door.

By the time Mr. Angry had made his way back to his property line, I had already run up the stairs and into our house to ask my dad what had transpired. It seemed that while measuring blades of grass—or some other equally unnecessary inspection of his property—Mr. A. had seen forensic evidence of animal activity. With a straight face, my dad then said he'd explained to our sour neighbor that they shared a common pest, "that same pesky squirrel" that had also been creating havoc on our property. That was Dad's story, and he was sticking to it. "The pesky squirrel." Even now, decades later, it still brings a tear to my eye and a knot in my throat as I recall those special days—how Jiggs taught himself covert operations and how my dad had my back. Always.

With a certain Australian terrier joining Jiggs as the only two dogs who had officially gotten under my skin, I found myself gravitating toward two Emme-related activities—dog walking and hiking. While living in Michigan, I had worked out at a gym two or three times a week, adding an occasional two- or three-mile walk on flat land on weekends. It felt like a good program for someone in his late fifties, especially given my workload at the office. But when I moved to the Woody Creek/Aspen area, not only were there no flat walks, there was also the thin air to contend with. Aspen sits at 8,000 feet above sea level, which just happens to be the level at which acute mountain sickness begins to occur.

The effects of high altitude were a non-issue for me until the day Pamela suggested that she and I go for a hike. The Michigan resident in me didn't take the word *hike* seriously at all, considering it a fancy name for a walk taken by someone who had just spent an hour dressing for the part at an Orvis store. But there is a reason why the St. Regis Aspen Resort employs a full-time "altitude concierge" to deliver personal oxygen machines to guests' rooms. Within a few minutes, I realized that a hike in Aspen was a completely different animal than any walking exercise I had ever experienced. Until this episode, I had considered myself in above-average shape for my age, and yet here I was, ten minutes up a small hill, first stopping and then sitting down to catch my breath. I thought to myself, *This is how it must feel to be a hundred years old.* It also made clear that I would need to adapt to my new home and significantly improve my fitness if I hoped to take part in so many of Aspen's year-round outdoor activities.

The local advice for adjusting to high altitude hiking is to take things gradually, which is how I found myself hiking on a brilliant August afternoon with Pamela and Emme on a moderately steep ski mountain in Aspen called Buttermilk. On our way down the hill, I spotted a large black bear at a lower point on the slope than us, maybe two hundred feet away. Being new to hiking the

Colorado mountains, this was the first time I had encountered a bear in the wild.

Since Pamela had lived in Aspen for seven years now, I deferred to my wife. After all, she was the "local."

"Okay, what do we do now?"

"Sing loudly," Pamela said, without hesitation. "That will usually make them go away."

Okay, I thought. *Usually? What about the times that aren't usual?*

Right off the bat, singing didn't strike me as an effective defensive weapon. Nor did the advice I recalled from the Don't-Feed-the-Bears brochures—*Make Sure the Bear Has an Escape Route.* What about the *humans* having an escape route? Unfortunately, the only way out for us was up the hill we had just climbed, and I thought I was not yet accustomed enough to hiking at 9,000 feet of altitude to be able to outrun a bear uphill. I even began to wonder if I should offer myself up as a distraction so that Pamela and Emme could escape. I recall hoping that if a few karate chops didn't do the trick, the bear would make fast work of me.

What would we do?

That's when Emme kicked into action. Displaying behavior best characterized as fearless yet totally crazy, she let out a series of high-pitched barks and bass-note growls, all the while running directly at the bear. My initial reaction to this confrontation was that it would only serve to infuriate the bear, who would then eat the barking puppy in a single gulp before coming for Pamela and me. I could imagine the headline in the *Aspen Times:* Newlyweds, Small Dog, No Match For Massive Bear.

Yet, astonishingly, the bear sprinted away. Weighing in at about the size of one of the bear's paws, Emme had chased the animal off the mountain path. Pamela called Emme to come back, she returned, and that was the end of the threat posed by my first up-close bear sighting in the wild. Still, just to make sure there wasn't another encounter, I began singing loudly and off-key, which is the only way I sing. We never saw our adversary for the remainder of the downhill hike—although I did imagine the bear hiding in the bushes and holding his ears. It was a performance Pamela later cited as the reason she has never suggested that I join her in karaoke.

History repeated itself a few weeks later while we were enjoying dinner outside at our Woody Creek property, which was not yet fenced in. As Pamela stood up to clear the dishes, she noticed that a particularly large black bear (probably over 300 pounds) had wandered into our yard. This time, instead of singing or running up the mountain, we quickly made our way into the house. And agreed *not* to answer the doorbell.

A bear at our Woody Creek home.

But before we could even take the plates from the table, we heard the unmistakable growl/bark and caught the sight of Emme again taking off after the bear. It was like a dog chasing a squirrel in that Emme was running at full speed, and the bear, lowering its body to the ground in a full gallop, shot out of our yard as though propelled by a jet pack. Black bears average about 275 pounds and can run—for a while anyway—at 30 mph. To put it in perspective, I did not own a car during my college days that could reach 30 mph. The futility of escaping an angry black bear spawned the joke about two men confronted by one of these creatures while in the woods. "Think you can outrun a black bear?" asked the first man. "No need," said the second man. "I just need to outrun you."

Let's recap—in her first summer with us, Emme had scared away two hulking black bears that were each fifteen or twenty times her size. The following spring, she would lead a cavalry of dogs out the back door and chase three bears up into an aspen tree that almost collapsed from their collective weight. Without a moment of hesitation, Emme had stepped up and displayed a level of courage (or craziness) I had never imagined a dog could possess on three different occasions. Okay, there were times we wished that she would use her superior canine IQ for higher purposes than figuring out how to penetrate the intricate packaging of any food she could reach by way of chairs, tables, and counters. But all things being equal, an acceptable amount of collateral food theft was a small price to pay for such an unexpected and beloved addition to the family—a supremely confident, independent-minded, outdoor-loving, and fearless young dog.

What would be the next adventure for our bear-chasing, fly ball-catching, puddle-hopping, SUV-navigating, home-protecting ten-pound precocious alpha puppy?

It would begin with a phone call from Portland, Oregon.

CHAPTER 3

BEST IN SHOW

"God loves a terrier."

—Sung by Gerry and Cookie Fleck, *Best in Show*

Emme with a major dog show win.

I t would be an understatement to say that Emme's first six months as self-appointed CEO of our Woody Creek home had been eventful. Australian terriers were bred to be "ratters and hedge hunters," and our diminutive puppy certainly fit that profile. From the moment she arrived, she believed it was her full-time job to protect her family from all members of the animal kingdom.

In the middle of my questioning whether the world might be ready for a remake of *Lassie* in the form of a bear-chasing, ten-pound bundle of guard dog, we received a phone call offering Emme her big break in a different kind of show business—the *dog show* business. It was Emme's breeder from Portland, asking for our permission to enter nine-month-old Emme in a weekend of Denver-area American Kennel Club (AKC) dog shows that would be taking place in August.

Except for having seen Christopher Guest's hilarious mockumentary film *Best in Show* about a year earlier, Pamela and I had no idea of what an honest-to-goodness, unscripted dog show involved. She had worked with an established breeder of Australian terriers only because her research had laid out the risks of buying from puppy mills and backyard breeders. And as Pamela pointed out during the "executive search" that brought us Emme, our best chance for a healthy dog was demanding one with a documented pedigree from the AKC. Completely trusting the breeder to look out for Emme on this trip, and out of gratitude for her providing us with our indispensable third family member, Pamela agreed.

We later learned that it is rare for a dog to be entered in a dog show and not go through any advance training in the basics—how to walk on the left side of the handler, how to stack (posing for a judge's appraisal), and how to move around the show ring. But when the breeder arrived, there were no dog show lessons, just nonstop grooming. It looked like the afternoon before the senior prom as the breeder pulled, plucked, and combed Emme's shaggy coat, an activity Emme generally tolerated but didn't appear to enjoy. And there was no mistaking our puppy's expression of complete befuddlement when, following the beauty treatment, she was placed inside her familiar travel crate for a trip the rest of the family would not be making.

Many of us have seen dog shows on television, but few of us know how they work or how they originated. Here's a quick summary. Purebred dog competitions like the Westminster Kennel Club Dog Show and the two AKC events Emme entered that weekend are called conformation shows. Although the event takes on the feel of a competition, the dogs are really being judged on how closely they *conform* to the written standards of their specific breed for appearance, gait, coat, ears, teeth, and temperament. Several of the written standards for individual breeds clock in at upwards of 1,000 words, with several going so far as to detail specifications for the breed's tongue color.

Originally an add-on to a famous poultry show that took place in Newcastle upon Tyne (UK) in 1859, dog shows grew in popularity in England, eventually making their way to the United States following the Civil War. Although continually being reviewed and revised, much of the same language for breeds' standards written in the late nineteenth and early twentieth centuries is still in use today, with each entrant theoretically judged against a platonic ideal of the breed. In short, the rules of a dog show should favor the Australian terrier that is the most "Australian terrier-ish," based on the most current AKC published guidelines for the breed.

The reason for the background information on dog shows is because Emme won. And she didn't win just once—she hit the trifecta, taking home three wins in three days in her class (Puppy six months to under nine months). Because the American Kennel Club makes available a permanent online record (it looks like the back of an old baseball card) of participation in AKC-sanctioned events, I can tell you that she won at the Australian Terrier Club of Colorado in Denver on Friday, August 17, 2001, then won separate Saturday and Sunday shows at the Greeley Kennel Club "Classic" Dog Show, about sixty miles north of Denver. And while they might not have been Westminster or Beverly Hills, the Greeley show had attracted hundreds of exhibitors and their dogs from all over the country. Emme—with the official AKC designation "Lucky Lady Emme"—had certainly shown well over the weekend in her class of "Junior Puppies" who were in the process of finishing their championships.

We had a good laugh after that first phone call telling us that Emme had won her class in the first show. After we received the call about her class win for the second time, Pamela immersed herself in every nugget of online information there was to glean about dog shows. After Emme was back home, the breeder confided to Pamela that she had entered Emme in these shows as "point fodder"—filling the class and breed with enough respectable "loser" dogs to win more points for the dogs entered for the purpose of finishing their championships. It began to make sense why there weren't dog show lessons for Emme—she had been entered to take the fall and, with it, earn a one-way ticket to Palookaville. Yet, she won her class in three different shows, resulting in what seemed like a carload of ribbons and a strong endorsement from the happy breeder that we had a serious show dog on our hands or, at the very least, a dog with an abundance of terrier temperament.

For her part, Emme seemed unmoved by the fanfare of her winning as she returned home the conquering heroine. In fact, rather than taking a victory lap or relaxing after what had to be a challenging three days in a high-stress environment, she dove back into her full-time jobs of protecting her family from the animals and reminding us not to leave packaged food within her reach. She also seemed especially charged up about every outdoor walk we took that week, as if to say—*Hey, Dad—let's not forget what's important.*

Then, September 11, 2001, happened, and it affected Pamela and me deeply. Emotionally, I was a wreck, alternating between being weepy for those who lost their lives, frustrated at being powerless to help, and angry beyond words that such an invasion inside the United States could even be carried out. Based on intense media speculation in those early days about the acts being part of a larger plan to target Jews, Pamela was vocal about our needing a second home in an isolated part of the world to which we could take flight if necessary. She had also left her executive advisor position by this time, so we had the flexibility to consider uprooting our lives if that's where the decision came out. Things progressed seriously enough that we visited Auckland, New Zealand, twice and placed a deposit on a home there. But when the purchase fell through, we realized that our extreme urgency to flee the United States had also subsided. By late November, we had returned to our normal living and regular day-to-day habits, although we carry forward the vivid and raw memories of September 2001 to this day.

Normal living meant that Emme and I were back to spending four or five days a week on the hiking trails—both the old familiar spots and some new ones that had become options after medium snowfalls. Having arrived in the world on January 31 and in Colorado on April 5, Emme had managed to catch only the tail end of the snow season, which averages 175 to 200 inches per year (the U.S. average is 29 inches). Our dog immediately embraced the snow, recognizing her new challenges and the opportunities for the sheer fun that it presented. Copying what she had recently begun doing on our river walks, she took the lead, which in the deeper snow meant hopping and diving into it to create new tracks. As long as the new snowfall accumulations didn't completely bury her—which was about seven inches in that first full winter—Emme ran out ahead into the fresh snow, rather than following along on a trail flattened by snowshoes as most dogs seem to prefer. Only when temperatures dipped below about five degrees Fahrenheit did she alternately lift her paws from the cold ground to show that she was uncomfortably cold and wished to return to the warmth of the indoors. Extreme cold was the only reason she ever passed up an adventure in the outdoors in all our days as hiking partners.

Over Presidents Day weekend 2002, I found myself making the three-and-a-half-hour trek from Woody Creek to Aurora, Colorado, to drive my loved ones—Pamela and Emme—to the Plum Creek Kennel Club "Classic" Dog Show. Pamela had resumed her education in how best to participate in the world of dog shows and taught herself the basics of grooming and handling so that Emme could be shown. The skill levels of a dog's handler, I was learning, could make all the difference in this world. In the words of one-time president of the Westchester Kennel Club, Peter Knoop—"A good handler can win with a dog another man might have trouble giving to his neighbor."

Although it might not sound like a glamorous weekend desti-nation, the Plum Creek show is presented by the largest all-breed AKC club in Colorado and regularly attracts over 1,000 entries. That this was a top-tier dog show was why Pamela and Emme were there. Trying to be a supportive and engaged spouse was why I was there. It also helped that I had never attended a dog show in my life and was always up for something new.

I hadn't bargained on this.

Dog shows are a world unto themselves. I saw an entire eco-system of dogs, the owners, the handlers, the judges, the local offi-cials, the venues—all mixed into an atmosphere of prepping and competition.

With little to contribute while Pamela groomed Emme, I toured the Arapahoe County Fairgrounds, intending to learn more about the inner workings of a real dog show. What stood out on that first day was the intensity of the exhibitors and their assistants, particularly in the preparation and grooming of their dogs. Tech-nically, no foreign substances are permitted to be used on dogs. Not only is this vague edict not enforced by the judges, there is something of an arms race, and it takes place out in the open. As one person pushing the rules once told me, "How can this be a for-eign substance? It's made in the USA." It is hardly front-page news that pretty much everyone uses hairspray, with dyes, gels, styling mousse, cornstarch, colored pigment, and hair extenders in rotation but not as obvious as the ubiquitous aerosol cans. White chalk and powders also seemed to be prevalent among those attending to the fur of white dogs, which tends to naturally turn yellow. (There would be no yellow hair at this show.) The only disqualifications I know of for a foreign substance violation occurred when a light pat to the dog's back produced a white puff that changed the color of a judge's dark suit.

Critics of football once estimated that for all the fanfare, pageantry, and highlights shown over a three-hour telecast, each game offers only between nine and eleven minutes of action. As I figure it, the low percentage of action is about the same for a dog show. Take a classic Westminster favorite, the standard poodle. It takes over three hours to bathe and dry a standard poodle, with another ninety minutes needed to meticulously prune these dogs with decorative hairdos that make them look like landscaped hedges. For all this buildup, the standard poodle gets maybe two minutes of jaunting around the ring, followed by the requisite and thorough manual examination by the judge.

I walked around at that first show in Aurora, mostly people-watching, after which I concentrated on the dogs. It's an unscientific and unproven premise that people unconsciously (or perhaps consciously) chose dog breeds that resemble themselves, and this setting provided substantial data with which to test out the theory. Surprisingly, when I gently confessed to the owners why I had chosen to photograph them, several of them said they'd already been told of the dog-human resemblance. In nearly every case, people were only too happy to pose for me with their look-alike dogs. I had briefly considered heading back to share my findings with Pamela and how she shared her reddish-brown hair color and regal, warrior-like demeanor with Emme. But not wishing to tempt fate and risk a four-hour ride from Aurora to Woody Creek in silence, I opted to save my observations to the "drafts" file.

On April 13 at the Terry All-Kennel Club Show in Brighton, Colorado, Emme won her first point toward championship status, winning first place for twelve- to eighteen-month-old dogs, and the winner among the various class winners. To attain champion status, a dog must accumulate fifteen total points at shows in its lifetime, including at least two majors of at least three points each under different judges. Owners of champion dogs may then begin to use the prefix CH before the official registered AKC names.

There was only one problem with our rising star on the dog show circuit—Emme didn't like dog shows any more than I did. And because she was a dog and couldn't scream, calmly argue, or create a PowerPoint, outlining the reasons she didn't care for dog shows, Emme used body language and—let's call it what it was—disruptive behavior.

The changes in her dog-show conduct started in May or June when she began to gently nip Pamela during the grooming sessions that preceded the festivities. Pamela says Emme was never nipping with intent to injure but more as though to say—*C'mon. Dog shows? Enough is enough.* Pamela wondered if the breaking point was the day Emme shared a tight grooming (and breathing) space with a Pekinese whose fur was augmented by several cans of hairspray.

Some regional kennel clubs scheduled their shows such that one weekend per month, there can be three separate shows within driving distance of one another, with two often being held on back-to-back days at the same venue. This made necessary three rounds of primping, prodding, and combing in three days, a schedule which likely became tedious for an alpha Australian terrier, a breed that tends to "bore easily," according to Dr. Pippa Elliot of the University of Glasgow. The nipping also coincided with Pamela suspending the extended hikes with Emme she had built into the dog show weekends due to lack of familiarity with out-of-town trails.

Emme's next level of defiance at dog shows took the form of leaping from a grooming table and making a break for an open door. Since she was far from the first of her species to see an open door as a path to freedom, there is a procedure in place where people shout, "Loose dog!" when an entrant takes off for sweet liberty. As you'd expect, she was focused and determined in her attempted escape, deftly dodging people and obstacles as she sprinted for daylight. But when her breakout plan broke down and left her staring at a locked door, Emme calmly turned herself in to the authorities.

But despite Emme's obvious disdain for dog shows, she managed to keep accumulating points. Pamela, however, could see the obvious difference in her enthusiasm levels between when she recognized the run up to a weekend dog show and when Emme and I were getting ready to take the SUV over to one of our hiking trails. It was the difference between watching your kid trudge off to school on a rainy Tuesday in March versus seeing the response to your spur-of-the-moment breakfast announcement that the family would be going to the circus.

As much as Pamela had taken to the world of dog shows, she entered Emme in just one weekend of shows between mid-August 2002 and mid-January 2003. For all her class wins and ribbons,

Emme had acquired just two of the fifteen points needed for her championship, and Pamela's thought at the time was to take some time off the circuit and make a run at Emme's championship in early 2003 by entering a fixed number of high-profile shows. Pamela had plans to continue showing dogs, but she knew that those shows would not include Emme. Our Aussie terrier had gone from running the table to running from the table. The latest line Emme had drawn in the sand was refusing to get out of her crate at a show. As I heard Pamela say to people dozens of times when asked if Emme enjoyed dog shows—"Are you kidding? She can't wait to get home and hike with her dad."

Pamela wasn't kidding about Emme's devotion to our hikes, particularly in the early fall of 2002. Our little dog had seen snow for the first time a year earlier, but this year she was ready, as though she had spent her entire summer waiting for the colder weather and the fluffy white stuff to return. Now larger and stronger as she approached her second birthday, she hit the trails with a renewed joy and intensity I wish I could bottle and drink down on those days when I didn't have a bounce in my step. If trying to escape from dog shows was her attempt to communicate how she felt about that activity, her sheer elation on the snowy trail spoke just as eloquently. There was also an element of *Look at how great I am at this* as she carried over her graceful style on walking paths to a completely different skill set of bringing her tracks to the fresh snowfall. And after following Pamela and me for about a month on those earliest walks along the river, she took the lead now every time the two of us hiked anywhere. As David Frei, the beloved former television commentator for the Westminster Kennel Club Dog Show, said about Aussie terriers—"It's their world, and we're just in it."

Emme loving the deep snow.

After a five-month "vacation" that included about a hundred hikes around our home but only one dog show (where she won a few more of her classes), Emme was back in with all four feet, starting the new year with shows in Washington State, Oregon, and Nevada. It was the beginning of an astounding run for my girls— on January 10, 2003, Emme and Pamela entered the Tacoma Kennel Club's show with just two points. Just eight days later, Emme had attained champion status. She had run up sixteen points in just four shows. She would forever be officially known as CH Lucky Lady Emme.

And with that, it was back to Emme's calling: hiking with her dad. Pamela, meanwhile, had gotten serious about dog showing. She enjoyed the preparation, the competition, the learning, and all of it with a dog breed she loved. Early in Emme's showing, Pamela read the tea leaves that she would need a new athlete to continue on. Enter Tucker, a gorgeous example of a male Aussie who matured into a great show dog. To our great fortune, Emme decided she loved Tucker, and they got along famously.

Although I had sworn off dog shows, I forced myself out of retirement to be in attendance in 2006 when Tucker, then a precocious two-year-old, was one of five select Australian terriers invited to take part in the 130th annual Westminster Kennel Club Dog Show at New York's Madison Square Garden.

It began when Pamela met the world-famous handler, Gabriel Rangel, at an Arizona dog show in which she had entered Emme and Tucker. Gabriel and his wife Ivonne, who was the only person ever to place an Australian terrier in the terrier group at Westminster, soon became Tucker's professional handlers. But while most dogs shown with professional handlers live for a period of time with those handlers, so they can bond outside the ring, Pamela couldn't deal with the dogs being away. So, Emme and Tucker continued to live at home with us, and Pamela traveled with them to shows where they would meet up with Gabriel and Ivonne. Although they usually showed our dogs in the breed, Gabriel and Ivonne would have so many winning dogs at certain shows that Pamela would sometimes step in and take Tucker into the group ring herself. The experience with the Rangels taught her to become one of the best owner–handlers in the breed.

The Westminster experience was one we would never forget.

First, ours was one of the few flights to land at JFK on February 12, as New York City was being buried by a snowstorm that dumped 26.9 inches in Central Park. This was the most snow ever recorded in New York City since recordkeeping began in the mid-1800s. The first blue ribbon of the week went to the United Airlines captain who landed the plane on a snowy, icy runway in minimal visibility.

Somehow, our cab made it to the Hotel Pennsylvania, the owner of New York City's phone number in longest continuous use and the title of a 1940 big band hit by Glenn Miller (Pennsylvania 6–5000). Those fun facts, and the hotel's location across Seventh Avenue from Madison Square Garden, were the only redeeming qualities of this "historic hotel that combines unique historic character and modern-day luxury." Upon entering the lobby, we quickly realized we were immersed in the thick of things, having booked the official hotel where most of the 3,000 participating dogs and their entourages had also secured lodging. The paper-thin walls gave us nowhere to hide from the continuous barking or, should I say, dogs communicating with one another.

Another challenge for us at the hotel was the natural bouquet of thousands of dogs, combined with pungent aromatics of canine waste, aerosol grooming products, and half-eaten liver treats. The hotel's minimalist approach to ventilation never had a chance. When I sensed the early signs of a splitting headache, the idea was to head downstairs in an attempt to clear my head and lungs with a whiff or two of frigid New York City air.

But as I made my way through the revolving door, I realized I would not be alone. Almost two dozen men and women (but mostly men) had braved the swirling snow and the heaviest of the record-breaking snowfall to stand under the Hotel Pennsylvania's Seventh Avenue heated awning. Finally, one of the men said to no one in particular, "I just needed to breathe." Another chimed in with, "I had to get out of there." Then sounds of general agreement came from five or six more of us. The doorman had informed us a couple of hours before that New York City's emergency laws had kicked in. "Essential vehicles only"—there would be no more cabs that night. But no one in our group was here to hail a cab. We were twenty people, brought to this hotel first by a love for our dogs, and at this moment drawn together in a collective search for a deep breath.

Even New York City couldn't make twenty-seven inches of snow disappear overnight, but there were wide pathways carved out for the short walk across the street to the Garden. When we got inside and were assigned a space for Tucker, it reminded me of the cantina scene in the original *Star Wars,* with hundreds of dogs on tables being combed, brushed, sprayed, painted, and everything else that is done at dog shows. And just as in the film, there were long noses, mashed noses, long hair, short hair, pom-pom hair, long tails, cropped tails, and curled tails. There were dogs that could see through their hair and others who couldn't possibly see given the amount of hair over their eyes. There were floppy ears and straight-up ears. All of them were yapping, whining, barking, and baying out different tunes. The cacophony was like hearing a hundred jukeboxes, all playing different songs.

As I tended to do at dog shows, I left Pamela to handle the grooming responsibilities while I went out sightseeing, given that there were probably a hundred breeds backstage at Westminster that I'd never set eyes on in my life. The star of the show for me was the Komondor, or Hungarian sheepdog. It had the Rastafarian look of a mop head with a tongue coming out of it, accessorized with a white-colored, rope-like fur coat made up of long, dense cords.

If there could have been a Best in Show in the owner category, it was the woman who had accompanied a Komondor into the doggie poop area. Due to the dog's dreadlocks "back there"—called cords, mats, and flocks in the dog show world—the Komondor's bodily functions became a cooperative effort with the owner. This amount of hands-on assistance struck me as a higher level of commitment than I could ever muster on a regular basis—and I consider myself to be a dog person. It was an example of someone so dedicated to a dog that she would do whatever it took—and in this instance, "whatever it took" required a level of participation I couldn't begin to imagine.

Scratching my head at why someone would ever choose such a high-maintenance breed and what possible purpose the thick corded fur could possibly serve, I decided to walk up and ask the dog's owner these questions—after the poop process had been completed.

"The thick cords protect the dog from wolf bites," she said. "Even a wolf's jaws can't penetrate that fur." It all made sense—the dogs came from Hungary where they guarded sheep from sharp-toothed predators. The coat also helped the sheepdogs to deal with cold weather, given that they did much of their work in open fields in frigid temperatures. I wanted to ask if her Komondor living in the United States had ever confronted a wolf's jaws in its lifetime but decided against it. The pooping and loud, gruff barking aside, however, the Komondor had slowly won me over. I found myself coming down with Hungarian sheepdog envy.

Fortunately for Pamela, there were no similar "maintenance" obligations with the Australian terrier breed. Still, this was Westminster after all, so Tucker and all the other Aussies still needed to be groomed and shaped for the overall ideal look of the breed the judge would be looking for.

After hours of sipping coffees and consciously avoiding the unhealthy food choices being offered by the arena's vendors, the time came for the Aussies to enter the show ring. The judge was Mrs. Cate Elizabeth Cartledge, one of the UK's top all-rounders who was passed for eighty-seven different breeds. To my untrained eye, all twenty or so dogs in the ring looked indistinguishable from one another, but the judge projected authority and clearly knew what she was doing. As Gabriel walked Tucker in, I tried to pick the winner. It's not 100 percent about looks and conforming to the breed, since the dogs' gaiting and stacking for the judge's examination also figured into the rankings. When dogs are the size of Aussie terriers, they are stacked on a table, after which the judge conducts a manual examination that would make your family doctor blush.

Now, the tension was rising, and it was because a decision was about to be rendered. The judge had all the Aussies walk around the ring again. Staring at the group for a long time, she then divided the Aussies into two groups. At this point I anticipated the group of dogs that would stay because the three dogs I considered to be just so-so were all assigned to one group. My instincts were right, and it came down to six dogs, a group that included our Tucker. The judge then took one final appraisal of each of the remaining Aussies. She then had them walk around the ring a third time, and as they walked, she motioned dramatically for one of the dogs to move to the front. It was not Tucker. But just as I expected her to make the grand flourish of pointing at "one, two, three" for the breed winner, best of opposite sex, and awards of merit, she then motioned for Tucker and Gabriel to move to the front of the lineup.

Seconds later, she pointed affirmatively "one," then "two," then "three," while waving the others off. *Tucker wins the Australian terrier Best of Breed at Westminster!* My phone immediately exploded nonstop for the next hour with congratulatory texts and calls from friends, mostly those back in Aspen. Then again when they saw Pamela take Tucker into the Group ring as they followed Tucker's special night on the USA Network.

Tucker winning the Best of Breed at Westminster,
February 14, 2006, shown by Gabriel Rangel.

A wave of emotion came flooding over me as though I were at my child's graduation. I was proud of Tucker, but the tears flowed for all the effort and hours of hard work Pamela had devoted to making champions of our dogs and finding a passion she loved. A big stage means pressure, and she and Tucker had "handled" everything that was thrown at them, including other handlers trying to throw them off along the way. And guiding Emme to championship status was also no easy feat, having to work with a dog whose show preferences were always to be "somewhere other than here." Pamela had found an activity that captured her mind and spirit, and she had succeeded at the very highest level of that world.

A friend had the best perspective about winning and losing at dog shows: "Just keep in mind—at the end of every show you're always going home with the best dog."

CHAPTER 4

EMME DELIVERS

Dogs are our link to paradise.
They don't know evil or jealousy or discontent.
To sit with a dog on a hillside on a glorious
afternoon is to be back in Eden, where doing
nothing was not boring—it was peace.

—Milan Kundera

Emme and her newborn puppies:
Tory, Enzo, Hunter, Ryder, and Tilly.

I t isn't a common occurrence to be able to walk off into the sunset on one's own terms as a newly crowned, once-and-forever champion. And it is even more unusual to accomplish this feat shortly after celebrating your second birthday.

Yet this was the résumé of our Emme—now known as CH Lucky Lady Emme (the CH for champion)—who, after a promising 2001 in which she took home a series of consolation ribbons but only one point toward her championship, put up seventeen points over the course of two weekends in January 2002. This meant she was finished. In the terminology of the American Kennel Club, "finished" meant earning the requisite number of total points (fifteen), six points in two majors, and nine points from enough different judges to qualify for the title "Champion of Record."

Emme was also finished because Pamela had decided to retire her from the dog show circuit. Our spunky and headstrong Australian terrier had made it abundantly clear that she no longer wished to participate in the primping, combing, trimming, and invasive squeezing of (dog) show business. Her body language and facial expressions at dog shows ranged from begrudging acceptance (*You know I don't enjoy this*) to outright revolt (*Get me out of here…now* and bolting for an open door). This was not to be confused with her behavior when she recognized that a hike was forthcoming, which instantly transformed her into the happiest and most enthusiastic dog I'd ever seen. When she'd calm down from the initial euphoria—which often took a while—or stare up at me from the console during the rides to our outdoor adventures, her message came through unambiguously—*This is more like it.*

But before retiring her to hiking trails, Pamela had one more calling in mind for Emme in 2002—motherhood. There had been much pressure and arm-twisting from the dog world for Emme's puppies since Aussies are still rare, and Emme's breeding would expand the gene pool. Now, at two years old, she was at an ideal age for breeding.

One important decision the owner must make on behalf of the dog that will be breeding is the identity of the sire, or father. When show-caliber dogs are mated, it's not carried out as a free-for-all at a dog park where paternity is determined by the results of a DNA test carried out by a daytime talk show. While Pamela later shared the unexpurgated details of Emme's arranged hookup, the best description for the purposes of this book is that it was *a process.*

Deciding on a sire turned out to be an easy call; Pamela's first choice was to use Tucker's sire. It turned out that the father's name was CH Ryba's Tom Foolery, he answered to the name Cisco, and he had availability in early February, which also worked for Emme's biological schedule. Also working in Cisco's favor was that he was ranked as the number one U.S. Australian terrier in the show ring at that time. My sense is that if you were put on this earth as a dog, it wasn't a bad deal to be Cisco.

Arrangements were made for Pamela and Emme to fly to the home of breeders Sue Bachman and Teresa Shreeder in Martinez, California, a town in the East Bay area about thirty-five miles from San Francisco. This was yet another benefit for sires with a proven track record—the collaboration with Emme would be a home game for Cisco.

As I have tried to spell out, Pamela's colorful and unvarnished play-by-play of the Australian terriers' mating ritual would jeopardize the G-rating our publisher recommends in bringing Emme's story to as wide an audience as possible. Suffice it to say that her detailed portrayal made the blessed event sound more like a game of Twister.

According to eyewitnesses on the ground, Emme "wasn't ready" and Cisco "wasn't really interested." While those words could have described a blind date gone bad, Emme's and Cisco's impasse reached three full days and counting. Patience has its rewards, however, and Emme and Cisco had successful breedings on the fourth and sixth days. After Pamela brought her home, the next step was to wait and see if Emme was pregnant. There is not yet an equivalent of a home pregnancy test for dogs, but an ultrasound after four weeks brought us the news Pamela had hoped for. If all went according to plan, Emme would be having puppies in April.

To no one's surprise, Emme was a "super trouper" (Pamela's words) throughout her two-month pregnancy—as fired up as always about hitting the trails and hiking almost every day at full speed until she was ready to give birth. In the final weeks of her pregnancy she even acquired a new obsession—swimming and playing with the fourteen koi fish that lived in a pond on our property. With koi said to be among the most intelligent of the fish species—and not just because they travel in schools—it was no surprise that within just a day or two, Emme and the fourteen fish had developed an elaborate game of tag. Measuring in at almost Emme's length, the koi fish would float along on the surface and either swim close or nudge her, making sure to dart out of range

when she lunged at them. The game so engrossed Emme that had
we not set aside time for hiking on those days, the games of tag
with the fish would have lasted around-the-clock.

Emme and her pond friends—koi fish almost her size.

The day arrived when Emme chose to remain behind in her
whelping box, and we knew that the delivery hour was at hand.
Specially made, it is like a nesting box, with sides high enough
to keep the newborn puppies in and lined with little blankets to
keep the pups warm. Emme knew exactly what it was for. It was a
couple of days later, on April 16 (and April 17), 2002, that Emme
became a mother.

Starting in the early evening, she began birthing her pups
at the rate of one per hour, the sight of the first three puppies
huddled closely around their mother was something I will never

forget. It was after number three that things slowed considerably, as Pamela speculated that we were likely in for a late night. It didn't matter because neither Pamela nor I would have been able to sleep anyway.

Because Emme was a first-time mother, Pamela had learned from vets and breeders that she needed to monitor things closely, particularly how the new mom was caring for her first two puppies. Called on to multitask, mother dogs are so fixated on giving birth to the next puppy that they sometimes take their attention away from the needs of the little ones delivered earlier who need to be kept warm and safe. (The room was kept quiet and at about eighty degrees Fahrenheit.) When the fifth and final puppy finally joined the festivities, it was after 3 AM, and exhaustion quickly replaced the adrenaline rush that had sustained us until that moment. As unobtrusively as we could, we generally cleaned what we could, replaced the bedding in the whelping box, and called it a night.

Common wisdom among breeders is that a female dog can be expected to be physically spent for up to twenty-four hours or more following the arduous process of giving birth to puppies. It is not unusual to find it necessary to lead a mother by a leash or carry her outside to resume bodily functions. Not Emme. After nursing her five pups on that first morning, she made her exit from the whelping box and gave the usual signal that she wished to go outside. Expecting to watch her walking gingerly after the eight-hour marathon that had ended just six hours earlier, you can imagine our astonishment when she made a beeline for the other side of the yard, leaped into the pond, and reacquainted herself with the fish. The game of tag resumed exactly where it had left off, with the koi fish all swimming up to Emme on the surface, then expertly avoiding her attempts to initiate contact with them. Emme had clearly been thinking for days about when she would be able to play tag again with her pals in the pond.

That Emme was able to summon the energy and stamina to dive in and begin swimming with the fish was a revelation for us. Still, Pamela called her right out of the water and immediately proceeded to bathe her. A thorough cleaning was needed to eliminate any risk of illness to the puppies due to bacteria or other germs that could be transferred from the pond. Just to be on the safe side, we kept Emme on a leash while she was on our property—and within sprinting range of the water—for the duration of the time she was nursing the pups.

Besides going for a swim on the morning after giving birth, Emme took several other unconventional approaches to her new responsibilities as a mother. For instance, each night she would make sure things were fine on the home front, nursing and cleaning them by dutiful licking. Once she checked those boxes, she would leave the little ones on their own, then vault over the protective gate and out of the puppies' room to sleep in our bed. Based on what we'd heard and read, this seemed to be (no pun) out-of-the-box behavior. Our experiences with subsequent litters would definitely corroborate that mommy dogs unfailingly stay in the whelping box with their puppies practically 24/7, at least for the first two weeks. New mothers tended to view other dogs and certain human visitors as predators, and all our mother dogs who followed would err on the side of being overly protective.

Not Emme.

When I ask Pamela all these years later for appraisals of Emme's maternal skills, the most optimistic words that she can muster are "okay" and "adequate." And she doesn't hesitate when I ask her which ones of her other females over the years have been better mothers than Emme.

"All of them," she answers.

I'm more of a glass-half-full evaluator. Emme's puppies all lived and thrived—that's saying something. And two of them were shown and became champions, another feather in her cap. And to her credit, she didn't become one of those modern helicopter parents who cloyingly micromanage every aspect of their young ones' lives. Her mothering instincts struck me as a nostalgic throwback to the loving, caring, but less hovering mothers of the '50s and '60s, who made our Long Island neighborhood such a great place to be a kid. Emme was old-school.

But even judged generously, Emme would sometimes take her expressions of tough love to extremes. When the puppies reached six weeks old, we began including them in hikes on our new favorite trail along a beautiful river. When the pups reached ten weeks, we advanced into rockier terrain. Once, after we had covered a short distance, the trail added a rocky scree on one side that sloped sharply up to a ridge. Hopping up-slope from rock to rock, Emme stopped on a ledge above, turned and invited the pups up to join her, which led to inevitable flopping and falling by the inexperienced little ones. Pamela would have no part of it, however, and called Emme down from the rocks in a demanding tone, which she deserved. Emme would then descend at her own deliberate speed and march on down the path looking for the next test. Emme had been an advocate of limited dependence since halfway through Day One, and her face on this day seemed to convey, *How long am I signed up for this motherhood job?*

Pups resting after an outdoor workout.

Pamela and I discussed what we both saw clearly in Emme's eyes. Anyone who tells you they can't understand what their dog is communicating simply isn't tuned into their dog. The record will show that April 16–17, 2002, would be Emme's first and final trip to the whelping box.

Later in 2002, Pamela decided to permanently retire Emme from further breeding and have her spayed. Her name—CH Lucky Lady Emme—would continue being added to breeding and progeny pages as her puppies, her puppies' puppies—and now her great-grandpuppies—have gone on to become champions, with American Kennel Club baseball-card bios of their own.

By the late spring, we were back in Colorado and had resumed a routine of hiking old reliable trails. As you'd expect from a dog that was able to sprint at full speed into a pond on the morning after she gave birth, Emme made a swift transition from the whelping box back to her familiar position on the console of the SUV, embracing our hikes with renewed vigor and purpose. As the post-puppy summer of nonstop outdoor activities drew to a close, Pamela recalls Emme's physical conditioning at age two-and-a-half as being "her muscles had muscles."

As for my own status, mid-to-late 2002 remained a transitional time for me. I was slowly picking up the pieces after the swift and surgical market corrections imposed by the tech bust and by the tragedy of 9/11. But the following summer, I would turn sixty—a mixed bag of a milestone but one that still offered enough remaining years that could add up to a third of my life. But it was also an age where I feared becoming a technology industry dinosaur. As for the skills I had acquired over the years, I now appreciated that the back nine of my life would require ongoing training, reinvention, and rebranding. Business experts were already estimating five to seven years as the half-life of specific skills before products and methodologies were sent off to the scrap heap. I needed to figure out the shifting landscape and choose my positioning in an increasingly digital world. Fortunately, my technology and management background was deep, which served as building blocks to become a strategic advisor to new-venture CEOs and to companies attempting to figure out how to succeed in a digital world.

It was in a spirit of lifelong training and exploring new ideas that I found myself curious about Pamela's next dog-related expedition, one that would take place in mid-September. After a friend of hers had suggested a two-week camp for dogs located in the Green Mountains of Vermont, Pamela had done her customary due diligence, and it checked all the boxes as a winner. The camp would represent a change of scenery for Emme and Misha, a new addition to our clan, a new set of hiking trails, encounters with unfamiliar species of wildlife, as well as full, scheduled days of supervised athletic activities and skill development for dogs. Reviews of the camp on the internet were great if you were a dog but did caution humans about the intensity of the dog lovers and the sketchy cell service in the mountains. But what the heck. Somewhere along the way, I heard myself blurt out the words, "I'm in."

Who could have known how those two weeks in the company of 250 dogs—and at least as many dog fanatics—would be such a game-changing experience for Emme and me and the catalyst for so much that would follow?

CHAPTER 5

CAMP COST-A-LATTE

*What's the good of living if you
don't try a few things?*

—Charles M. Schulz

*Pamela with Misha and Emme, and Janis with
Ruby and Cooper at Camp Gone to the Dogs.*

As doggie camp departure day inched closer, I was beginning to question my decision to accompany Pamela, Emme, and our second Aussie girl, Misha, on their wacky excursion to New England on September 12. "I'm in" felt like the right thing to say when I said it, but now that our departure date for camp was right around the corner, I was wondering what I'd gotten myself into. After all, I was looking at one full week—seven days, 168 hours, 0.03 percent of my life—with over two hundred dogs and at least as many dog-obsessed humans. Trying to devise an equivalent, I came up with being strapped into Disney's "it's a small world" boat ride, which would mean hearing the song "It's a Small World (After All)" more than 1,000 times a day.

In the end, I took one for the team, with the team being Pamela, the dogs, and me. Pamela appreciated my coming along, but she also sensed I could benefit from a "break in the action." It had been an intense year and a half since the tech bust, trying to rebuild our finances, which had meant significant time on the road and many hours in front of the computer. During that period, we hadn't taken a proper vacation, so we treated this trip as one—a complete change from our day-to-day life in Woody Creek and a full menu of activities for the dogs. To "ac-cent-tchu-ate the positive," Stowe, Vermont, was a glorious place to visit during September, with minimal rain, cool nights, lush green hills, and an average daytime high of 70 degrees Fahrenheit. As for transportation, we would be flying, at least to Boston, which covered 1,900 of the 2,100-mile trip.

Several months earlier, our friend, Janis Hearrell, had told Pamela about Camp Gone to the Dogs, which is the actual name of the camp and not another nickname I have assigned to it. Established twelve years earlier, the camp promised "a celebration of dogs and all the ways they bring joy into our lives." Based on Pamela's research, there was no doubt this experience would be an absolute blast for the dogs, with sixty to seventy different activities offered every day. Some of the offerings were lure coursing, Frisbee/K-9 disc, impulse control, Agility, Flyball, freestyle dance, and, of course, reading your dog's body language.

What we didn't count on was how serious the other campers were—and not just the humans. Many of the canine campers had done multiple tours of Camp Gone to the Dogs, and a good number of them had full-time, year-round trainers, particularly in Agility, which had become a separate category of regional and national dog show competitions. These doggie campers were already practiced performers who had come to Vermont to hone and perfect the fine points of their well-developed skills. When Pamela and Janis burst onto the scene with their dogs, who had received zero training in Agility, they said they felt like cowboys crashing black-tie Wednesday at the Broadmoor Waltz Club.

Campers (the dogs) and their owners could come for two weeks of festivities, but most came in for one week to moderate the cost. Pamela and I were only available for the first week. Janis, who was joined by her two Cavalier King Charles spaniels, was fine with that, as well. When we met up with her on the day before camp officially began, we took the dogs for a short hike up the main hiking trail in Stowe. Near the start of the hike we needed to cross a stream, which we did by tight-roping a log that was about a foot in diameter.

Emme and I made short work of it and had continued hiking when we heard Pamela yell out, "Emme, come back here and show Cooper how to do a water crossing." One of Janis's dogs refused to get up on the log and make the crossing, grinding our group outing to a halt.

Emme knew what was up. She left my side, danced back across the log, and stood in front of Cooper for a good ten seconds, delivering her now well-practiced and meant-to-be intimidating stare. She then turned and started walking deliberately, checking several times to make sure Cooper was still behind her, and slowly led him across the log. For his part, Cooper seemed to follow in an obedient trance. Safely on the other side—again—Emme appeared to grow wings, ran back to my side, and resumed the hike. Janis looked at Pamela, shook her head, and said, "If I hadn't seen that with my own eyes, I wouldn't have believed it."

My immediate objective on the first morning of camp was to find myself a decent bar—of cell service that is. This was the early 2000s, when Wi-Fi availability was a fraction of what it is now, and cell coverage was spotty, particularly in rural and mountainous areas. In this instance, the Green Mountains played havoc with mobile service, and it was no easy task to come up with the one or two bars my phone required for me to keep up with work communications. This is when I came up with the idea of driving to cell service, a trip I decided to combine with what became a daily coffee run. My mission, when I decided to accept it, was to (1) find the nearest Starbucks, (2) take advantage of their cell signal, and (3) get the order right for Pamela, Janis, and a group of their new pals. How tough could that be?

After a longer-than-advertised ride down the hill and into a neighboring town thirty minutes away, I finally located the

Starbucks. Fifteen minutes on a comfortable stool with three or four bars on the phone allowed me to catch up with those work emails and texts that required prompt attention. Step two would be to order the coffees, the specifics of which Pamela had provided on a sheet of paper I had yet to examine. It immediately struck me that although I considered myself to be a man of the world, I was not conversant in a foreign language known as "Starbucks-ese."

Order number one was so over-the-top that even all these years later, I can recite it from memory: "Grande Vanilla Bean Crème Frappuccino in a Venti cup, no ice, with caramel drizzle. With room for foam." At first glance I swore it read "camel drizzle," but then figured that can't be possible, even at Starbucks. As the barista took the order in stride, I felt as though I were back in Paris, ordering dinner by reading a page from the dictionary and wondering if the waiter would bring snails or a chair. The calm face of the barista gave me confidence that things were under control. Next—"Skinny iced caramel macchiato, upside down, extra caramel." I silently scolded the person back at camp who ordered this one, making a note to point out later that starting the order with "skinny," that is, fat-free, didn't make up for all the sugar that came after. And wasn't "Macchiato" the actor in *The Karate Kid?* The barista was still cool. Then—"Venti iced skinny hazelnut macchiato, sugar-free syrup, extra shot, light ice, no whip." Reading the drink names was taking so long I was in danger of missing the camp's dinner bell, and that was seven hours away. Finally, I made the executive decision to order seven venti vanilla skim lattes and hoped no one would notice.

Then I figured I owed one to myself. And I'd keep it simple. Yet after I had been perfectly understood in this seemingly foreign tongue, the final drink order produced the only blank stare of the entire transaction.

I asked for a regular coffee.

With apologies to Abbott and Costello and Steve Martin in *L.A. Story,* I can attest that the conversation went almost exactly like this:

Barista: *What do you want in it?*
Me: *Coffee.*
Barista: *Do you want room for cream?*
Me: *No, just room for sugar.*
Barista: *What size?*
Me: *Small.*
Barista: *You mean tall.*
Me: *No, I mean small.*
Barista: *Tall is small.*
Me: *I thought small was small.*
Barista: *(Silence)*
Me: *Then what is a medium?*
Barista: *Grande.*
Me: *But doesn't "grande" mean "large" in about two or three languages?*
Barista: *Large is venti. Grande is medium.*
Me: *Then how about the size smaller than medium?*
Barista: *That's tall.*
Me: *I'll take it.*

Not long after that, since I had plenty of free time, I did some research. It turns out this alternative language is the result of a trip to Italy taken by Howard Schultz, the one-time chairman and

CEO of Starbucks, in 1983. Impressed by what he saw and heard, he sought to incorporate the rich traditions of that country's coffee house culture into a newfangled coffee company that he had in the works. And proprietary, Italian-sounding sizing names were apparently part of the culture he sought to assimilate. Venti, for instance, means "twenty," which I guess was close enough for their 24-ounce drink. The Starbucks name itself comes from the moniker of the only crew member in Herman Melville's *Moby Dick* who tried to talk Ahab out of hunting the white whale. I came across a rumor that the company had considered the name of Ahab's whaling ship—the *Pequod*—but "a cup of Pequod" must not have worked for the focus groups.

As though this weren't enough, while making my way back to the main gathering area, I then witnessed a scene—G-rated, fortunately—that caught me off-guard, even at Camp Gone to the Dogs: owners were dancing with their canine companions. It struck me as a cross between a Fred Astaire Dance Studio and the Mos Eisley Cantina from *Star Wars*. Imagine dogs of all different shapes, sizes, and colors, standing upright on their hind legs with front paws in the hands of their human dance partners. The owners of the shorter dogs had a bit of a reach. I had to put down the coffees carefully, having become so engrossed that I was on the verge of dropping everything—and after all that driving, I needed to return with the grande vanilla bean crème Frappuccino in the venti cup.

As I eventually discovered, this was not an event hatched by the camp counselors but training for an actual circuit of performance competitions. Apparently, you can train with your dog for competitive, canine freestyle events that are conducted around the globe, much like dog shows and dog Agility competitions. There have even been dancing-with-dog performances on the TV show *America's Got Talent* that made Simon Cowell rise from his chair for a rare standing ovation. However, not all who participate in the dancing lessons at dog camp are aiming at formal competitions. Dogs want to please their owners, and they love to work. Owners enjoy having varied activities with their dogs and especially love when their dogs learn to respond to verbal and nonverbal communication. I've since seen YouTube videos of dog-human dance routines that are nothing short of incredible.

Once I adjusted to what was taking place, I could appreciate that every participant on the floor—human and canine alike—had been at this for a while. The humans seemed to be following their own rehearsed dance steps, while the dogs, to their eternal credit, did their best to keep things in play and appear agreeable. It reminded me of the old line about Ginger Rogers doing everything Fred Astaire did—only backwards and in high heels. Maybe *Dancing with the Dogs* would be the next big thing. I do know that I have rarely seen happier people. And they had clearly checked their pretensions and self-consciousness back at the Vermont state line.

After I delivered the still-warm coffee drinks that were enthusiastically consumed by all, we came up with an alternate plan that I'd make subsequent trips to a coffee shop located closer to the camp. The tradeoff was fewer choices (essentially "large latte with skim milk") for the possibility of my making two coffee runs. For my daily trips, I earned the title "Latte Boy" for the rest of the week, which was fine by me. I have been called worse.

By the time I got back from that first Starbucks excursion, Pamela had already decided that, training credentials be damned, she was going to put the dogs through as many of the doggie athletic exercises as possible. Emme put us into hysterics with her interpretation of Agility, where a dog negotiates miniature bridges, ramps, and tunnels, then weaves around pylons in a sequence that requires precise, hairpin turns. Focused solely on her own performance, she would sometimes attack the obstacles in the correct order, and sometimes she addressed the layout in a style all her own. She would sometimes look over at me after an incredibly skillful but out-of-order dash through the Agility course with a look that shouted, *But my approach made more sense.*

Our other Aussie terrier, Misha, was a willing participant in everything the camp had to offer, but she was more of a conventional Australian terrier female. It wasn't that she didn't take to the regimen of exercise and outdoor time, as she fully participated in activities she was seeing for the first time in her life. But she didn't turn every game into her personal Olympics, as Emme did, nor did she growl and stare down dogs that were three times her height for the sport of it.

Emme's favorite activity: bossing other dogs, no matter their size.

In her due diligence, Pamela had learned that an Aussie terrier does better with a companion than as an only child—and doesn't require 24/7 attention from its owner. So Misha was brought in to ride shotgun with Emme, and they had been fast friends from the day Misha arrived.

Speaking of our alpha female, Emme's challenge later in the day was lure coursing, which turned into her favorite end-of-the-day activity during the week. It's a bit like greyhound racing, where the dogs chase a white plastic bag about a foot off the ground—the lure—which looks to dogs like a speedy rabbit. Meant to teach dogs to hunt by sight rather than scent, the lure is pulled on a rope remotely by an experienced operator at a speed that, ideally, should just barely exceed the dog's maximum running speed.

Except the operator's experience had not prepared him for Emme. The first time we released her from her leash to chase the moving "rabbit," she darted after the lure—and immediately caught it. Onlookers sounded stunned, saying things like, "I'm not sure that was supposed to happen" and "I haven't seen one of those since that crazy beagle in 1996." The operator had evidently underestimated Emme's foot speed, based on profiling both her overall size and her short legs. It was a mistake he would not make again. Once the "rabbit's" speed was kicked up a notch, Emme fully embraced this game, as she stretched out into a horizontal streak with every intention of catching and finishing off the fake bunny lure. At the end of her run, they would let her get it, which resulted in a violent head shake that I have seen her use to kill real rodents and snakes. Once she deemed it "dead," she would casually place the white bag on the ground and proudly walk away.

Emme attacking the lure.

But the game in which Emme made the most impact and improved each day that week was Flyball. It was a relay race for dogs that involves a round trip of clearing hurdles, catching a tennis ball shot upward from a spring-loaded box, and activated by a lever the dog must press, and then returning to the starting line/ finish line with the ball in their mouth. Initially popularized by an appearance of inventor of the Flyball box, Herbert Wagner, on *The Tonight Show Starring Johnny Carson* back on November 4, 1976, Flyball held its first U.S. tournament in 1983, with large tournaments and championships held since then around the country, as well as in Europe and Australia.

A tireless thrower and catcher from her early days in our living room, Emme brought those same skills and a natural sense of timing to the game of Flyball. Upon clearing the hurdles, she would press the lever to shoot the ball straight up from the Flyball box, crouch, and then wait for the ball to hit the highest point in its arc and start falling, as the experienced Flyball-playing dogs already knew how to do. Only then would Emme jump to nail the ball at the highest point of her jump and start the return trip, dashing back over the four hurdles to the finish line.

Flyball relay teams of four dogs are not assigned by breed or by size, so the loophole in the game is the height of the hurdle being determined by the height of the shortest dog on the team minus five inches (e.g., if the shortest dog on the team is fourteen inches, that team would be given nine-inch hurdles). A short dog as a teammate would mean lower hurdles, but the equalizer is that most short-legged dogs cover too little ground in comparison to the longer-legged breeds to be regarded as competitive partners for mixed-size Flyball teams. But as the lure-coursing operator quickly found out, Emme was a super-fast runner. And her height was determinative of the height of her team's hurdles—almost. She was eleven inches high, but since the minimum height was then eight inches (now seven inches), Emme's team would always get the lowest hurdle setting. Even at eight inches, hurdles were no problem for Emme—she quickly mastered the game, as catching the ball and clearing the hurdles in both directions became a breeze.

A perusal of the camp's website these days emphasizes that four-legged attendees of all ages and skill levels are welcome, provided that behavioral issues are left outside the gates. But the makeup of the camp was different in 2002, when almost all camper dogs checked in with specialized talents their owners were looking to further refine by spending two weeks with the best instructors in the country. This made us even more proud of our dogs. They might have begun the week as party crashers, but by the seventh day they not only fit in with the other campers but were starting to flourish. And while I will freely concede a home-team bias, Emme stood out as the most exciting Flyball player in the camp, if only because she had found a way to excel as a short-legged dog in the long-legged dogs' games. Watching her six-inch legs easily propel her over the hurdles drew occasional *ooh*'s and *ah*'s from the spectators, and her take-no-lip Type A attitude won her the healthy respect of the camper quadrupeds.

Besides our dogs' athletic achievements, our week in the lush mountains of Vermont produced this partial list of observations, discoveries, and developments:

- There was a single, large boulder on the grounds of the camp that, when climbed to its highest point, provided two bars of cell service—as long as one could maintain balance;
- Emme and I thoroughly enjoyed hiking the area's unfamiliar trails. Every mountain has something to teach, and this applies double for the Green Mountains; and
- Dog owners truly love their dogs and not only want them to excel in activities designed for dogs, but also love engaging with them intensely—all day and for days in a row.

As we gathered with the other owners for customary end-of-week turkey dinner, this skeptic had been converted. Camp Gone to the Dogs had turned out to be a pretty special place. The teachers and instructors were knowledgeable, effective, and unfailingly positive in their interactions with the dogs and with people. The word used most often by the camp's instructors is the same one used most often in the online promotion—"fun." As in "If it's not fun for your dog, we won't do it." By the time you're packing to go home, you realize that they have walked the talk—everything about the camp is done to provide enjoyment for the dogs, and everybody there is rowing in the same direction.

Fun was also a general vibe caught by the passionate owners, nearly all of whom were collegial and supportive, as opposed to the dog-eat-dog (sorry) competitiveness of the dog show crowd. Camp folks were competitive, for sure, but their reaction to the success of other's dogs was usually appreciation, humor, and, more often than not, congratulations. It helped that most of them appeared to be having the time of their lives. Did I mention that later in the week, I stumbled upon a mixed-species square-dancing class?

You arrive in camp believing you're at a place that allows dogs; when you check out you realize you've just spent a week at a camp for dogs that allows people.

While I can fully appreciate the enjoyment of passionate and competitive dog owners, my own view is that the fun of dog ownership has more modest ambitions, such as having a companion on a hike or a thirty-minute game of catch in the yard. That was my last dog camp, but I learned there are many repeat campers who make the annual pilgrimage from all corners of the country to the unique experience offered in the Green Mountains. This has included Pamela, who has driven with a canine contingent from Colorado to Camp Gone to the Dogs—and back home again— nearly every September since our first such "vacation."

It didn't hurt that Emme, who wanted only to explore new hiking trails when we first arrived, quickly warmed to the athletic activities back at that first camp. And as the week progressed and Emme's skills and speed became apparent, the other dog owners and instructors noticed her mettle and noticeably warmed to her. We arrived at camp knowing that her footwork, instincts, and sense of direction—and no real competition—made her the best hiker in our family. But by week's end we saw—and heard from others—that she stood out among her class of 200 trained and talented dogs from all over the country.

While Emme had fun in some of the activities, Pamela, saw right through that. She said she knew exactly where Emme wanted to be and what she wanted to be doing. And it wasn't catching pop-ups or chasing fake rabbit lures.

"It's obvious," she said. "All she wants to do is hike—with you."

Clearing the hurdles by a mile.

CHAPTER 6

TAKE ME HIGHER

The mountains are calling,
and I must go.

—John Muir, "Father of the National Parks"

Emme at the summit. She always wanted to go higher.

I n the months following our arrival home from Camp Gone to the Dogs, Emme's affinity for mountain hikes grew from animated joy to unbridled exuberance. She'd become so flipped out about an imminent hike in those days that her frenzied behavior reminded us of Bugs Bunny's cartoon pal, the Tasmanian Devil. If I so much as picked up my hiking boots, backpack, or Emme's orange vest, she would immediately race to the door leading to the garage. Moreover, once she sensed that hiking preparations had begun, she would shut down eating. Not even food was more exciting than being out on the mountains. We were careful to make sure she was fed before I'd give the slightest hint that we were about to embark on a hike.

We had just added her orange vest to our hiking gear because it made it easier to spot her visually on the bare tundra and in the snow. But to Emme it meant so much more. She had the vest, and it announced to the world that she was special. Watching Emme beam with pride reminded me of every eight-year-old kid trying on their first Little League uniform and how important it makes them feel. There was something about putting on that uniform that suddenly made all things seem possible.

The orange hiking vest was Emme's "uniform," and she loved it. She would stand perfectly still but breathing hard with anticipation while I fastened the snaps. Upon hearing the final snap, she would start jumping around again, waiting for the door to open, so she could jump into the 4Runner. Once inside, she would assume the same statue-like position on the armrest she'd taken since our earliest walks along the Roaring Fork River.

As we stepped up the duration, variety, and altitudes of our climbs that fall, Emme made it known that wherever we happened to be hiking was exactly where she wanted to be. It also seemed that wherever we went, she would try to find the highest rock or mound to climb on, as though she had an instinct for summiting. The longer hikes also gave me more time to think—and learn. Watching Emme continue to master all aspects of hiking and exploring the outdoors reminded me how cool it is to discover a passion and be able to go for it. Up to this point, my life had been a series of these passions, both in my personal and business lives. Listening to and following my heart was when I felt most alive. Unfortunately, some of this flame was extinguished as I reacted to the tech bust and the impact it had on our lives financially. My network of business connections and personal friends was helping to lead me to new opportunities, but I was still in the plodding phase—at best. By far, the best part of those days was hiking with Emme. More than simply distracting me with her skills and antics, she brought a happiness that filled the air to our time together on the trails.

A hike I won't soon forget took place over that winter with our good friends Dexter Cirillo, her husband, Dr. Dennis Cirillo, and their two Parson Russell terriers. A handsome breed that is mainly white with brown markings, the Parson Russell terriers had legs that looked to be twice the height of Emme's, with a gazelle-like stride that made it appear that the dogs were floating through the air while running. Like the Russell and the Jack Russell breeds of terrier, the Parson Russell terrier is also named after the Reverend John "Jack" Russell (1795–1883) who, when he wasn't tending to his flock at church, loved to hunt foxes in and around his hometown of Devonshire, England. He developed a soft spot for hunting dogs and went on to become one of the most recognizable names in the history of dog breeding.

Emme got along well with the Parson Russell terriers, although our first hike with the Cirillos brought out Emme's Greatest Hits—growling into the faces of the two dogs, then staring them down with her signature intimidating glare. This resulted in the female, Filomena, flipping over on her back and submitting and Luigi, the male, walking away, wanting no part of an argument or whatever else Emme was up to. Conceding alpha dog status to Emme worked out for all sides, as the growling and staring gave way to a genuine comradery among the dogs as they became frequent hiking partners.

On this chilly winter morning Dexter, Dennis, the three dogs, and I were walking up one of the most scenic roads in the country, Maroon Creek Road, which starts at the traffic circle entry to Aspen and gains 2,100 feet of elevation over nine glorious miles, topping out at Maroon Lake and stunning mountain views. It is especially attractive for hiking when it is closed to auto traffic about halfway up through the winter due to the deep snows and avalanche risk at its higher altitudes. In addition to the aspen groves and almost too-perfect snow scenes, the road also offers glimpses of the majestic Maroon Bells, cited at one time by Kodak as the most photographed mountain peaks in the United States.

As we continued ahead, we came upon a steep drop from the left side of the road that led to water far below. The snow on the road had been cleared and patted down by snowmobile traffic, but the soft and loose snow was easily three feet deep on the slope, heading sharply downhill to the gully and Maroon Creek, which runs parallel to the road. As much as Emme loved to make new tracks in the fresh snow, three-foot powder was too much to handle for a dog whose head reached to about seventeen inches off the ground. Three feet of snow was even over the heads of the Parson Russell terriers, whose heads probably measured in at twenty-three or twenty-four inches.

The numbers all made sense—stay on the road. But no one told the dogs.

At the same moment all three dogs caught sight of an animal at the bottom of the slope near the river, and before we could react, they took off like a shot. The Parson Russell terriers are extremely fast and used the momentum from jumping off the road down the steep slope to create a channel and push through the snow. By the time we realized what was going on, Filomena and Luigi were down at the river and head-butting into a bush, where we'd guessed the outnumbered animal had sought emergency cover. Helped along by the twin snowplows that preceded her, Emme also made it down to the bottom, although she was uncharacteristically hanging back and watching. It struck me as unusual behavior for the alpha dog that prided herself on being first into every fray.

Dennis and I looked at each other and knew immediately that there was no way the dogs would be able to climb back up the slope. The snow was recent, fluffy, and deep, and the slope would be too steep for the dogs to climb. They had reached the river only by riding gravity and the steepness of the hill—which worked in only one direction. We had no choice. A little more than halfway down the slope in the waist-high snow, I wondered how the five of us would make it back up to the road. By this time Dennis had already plowed all the way down and reached the dogs. And he shouted words you don't want to hear.

"It's a porcupine," he said. "Stay there. I need to get the dogs up to you."

Five minutes ago, we had a situation. Now, we were in crisis mode.

I called out to Emme, and she struggled mightily to almost swim up the slope. Waist-deep in the snow, Dennis helped by grabbing and throwing her, which moved her about five feet closer to me. With about ten feet to go, Emme and I each covered enough ground to meet in the middle.

Emme had exactly two porcupine quills stuck in her and no more. One was in the top of her head and the other in her neck. I needed to exercise extreme care in pulling them out. The quills are so dangerous because they pierce the skin more easily than an eighteen-gauge hypodermic needle and have backward-facing barbs that prevent the quill from being removed without inflicting serious pain and significant damage to surrounding tissues. Another complicating feature of the quills is that they regularly break off, leaving pieces under the skin of the porcupine's attacker, which work themselves deeper with each muscle contraction.

It can be distressing for a dog owner to pull quills straight out because, while this method gives one the best chance for complete removal, it will cause the dog to flinch and yelp in pain. But Emme made it easy. When she finally reached me, still only halfway up the slope and covered in snow, she stopped in her tracks, braced herself on her four legs, and stared up at me. *She wanted me to pull the quills.* Going first for the one in her head, I grabbed the quill at its base where it had entered her skin, pinched hard, yanked quickly, and out it came. Emme never shied away or made a sound. She just kept staring at me—there was one more to go.

Things went the same with the quill in her neck—out it came, and not a sound or a movement from Emme. This was the same dog who would howl, yank her feet away, and faux-bite people's hands when she was on a grooming table at a dog show at the slightest tug of a comb through her fur. But here she stared down sharp pain without so much as a flinch—as long as we were on an adventure and out in the wild.

With both quills safely removed, Emme was ready for the rest of the trip, which was probably another twenty feet. I threw her about five or six feet up to a spot where she was able to fight and swim the rest of the way up to Dexter, who fully extended to reach her and place her on the road.

Next up was Filomena, and she was in extremely bad shape. Dennis had slogged uphill with her, until he was within throwing range of me. When his dog landed nearby, I had a close-up look at how porcupines protect themselves from predators. Quills were sticking out everywhere—not only from the poor dog's skin but inside her mouth, up her nose, and from her gums. She resembled a living pin cushion, and it was difficult for me to even look at her. But we needed to get her up to the road, so I grabbed her under her stomach—the only place on her body with no quills—and pushed her up the slope until reaching a spot where I could throw her to Dexter. Still shaken by the sight of Filomena, I headed back down for Luigi, who would represent the final leg of the up-the-steep-slope relay.

The deep snow and dealing with the hill began to take its toll on Dennis and me, but we did catch two breaks in our final dog transport. Luigi had about half the quill count Filomena had, although it was still too many for us to deal with on the scene.

(Also, Luigi wanted no part of quill removal, yelping and squirming as I managed to remove a few of them.) The second break was that in the two trips up to Dexter with Emme and Filomena, I had managed to kick steps into the snow, making it easier to carry Luigi up without sliding backwards. I didn't even have to throw him to Dexter. By the time Dennis followed us up the slope, the deep trough we left behind looked like a pock-marked luge course that ran to the creek.

After handing off Luigi, my first instinct was to check Emme for quills one more time, and I found none. She had clearly gotten the message that attacking the porcupine was a questionable plan. The porcupine issues a series of warnings for all the senses—a clicking of teeth, a spiny display of its tail and chest, and a pungent, unique-to-the-species odor—to let predators know that the quills are in place and ready to be deployed. Maybe Emme received the porcupine's alarms, while the Parson Russell terriers, known as highest-energy hunters among the three breeds named for Reverend Russell, acted on the sights and smells for "fat," "slow," and "rodent" (the porcupine is the third-largest rodent). My guess is that Filomena and Luigi didn't register "porcupine" until it was too late.

Getting the two injured dogs up to the road had taken a major effort and left Dennis and me exhausted. But it was obvious to all of us—and especially to Dennis as a plastic surgeon—that our job was only half-done and that we needed to get his dogs to a veterinarian as quickly as possible. My strong advice about dealing with porcupine quills is that unless you are far from civilization or dealing with a handful of quills or less, take your pet directly to a veterinarian. Now that we had climbed back up the slope with our dogs, the next challenge would be hiking the three or four miles back to the cars while carrying Filomena and Luigi.

Fortunately, it was precisely at that moment that a group of snowmobilers approached from farther up Maroon Creek Road. With intense focus and emotion, Dennis flagged down one of the guides and made clear that we needed their help. It reminded me of one of those scenes in the movies where the driver is pulled from his vehicle by the hero, who usually flashes a badge of some kind and says, "I am taking your car!" There is no doubt Dennis would have eventually delivered a version of that same speech had the guide not immediately snapped into action by radioing his base command, which caused a snowmobile towing a giant sled to materialize in a couple of minutes. Dennis climbed into the sled with the two stricken dogs, while another member of the group drove Dexter back to the parking lot in his snowmobile. Emme and I wound up hiking back to the parking lot, giving me plenty of time to reflect on the action-packed day we'd just experienced and how Emme somehow knew to stay away from that porcupine.

I learned later that the two dogs had to be anesthetized for the extractions to be performed, with the vet visibly shaken by the extent and location of the quills. Dennis, as the founder of the Aspen Institute for Plastic and Reconstructive Surgery, asked for and was granted permission to assist with his dogs' quill extractions. There were so many quills inside both dogs that the obvious ones were covering others that were either shorter or which had already broken off. The final count was ninety-six quills for Filomena, including one in her eye that Dennis was able to remove without any lasting damage to her vision. Luigi had about half as many, which still represents a major challenge for the vet and prolonged treatment for the animal. Some of the quills that had broken off took months to work their way to the skin's surface and required that the Cirillos perform daily exams of their dogs. In all, it took several more extractions and two additional surgeries under anesthesia over the next six months before the vet pronounced Filomena and Luigi quill-free.

Based on what I later read about porcupine quills, I made a mental note to add a multi-knife with pliers to my hiking kit in the event of future encounters while hiking out in back country. Dogs who make it to a vet's office usually survive even the worst of porcupine confrontations, but I could envision times when it may be imperative to get the quills out on the mountain or in the backwoods. (I subsequently had this experience twice—once with Tucker and once with a friend's dog—where the pliers came in plenty handy.) The good news is that Filomena and Luigi are two cases of dogs who survived serious wounds because they received prompt medical help—from both the veterinarian and their plastic surgeon owner. I can also report that we joined the Cirillos, Philomena, and Luigi on regular local hikes, and it was a joy to behold the Parson Russell terriers' graceful running style and enthusiasm for the outdoors. But I will not soon forget that eventful winter day on Maroon Creek Road, and you will never hear me refer to a porcupine as "cute."

Sometimes I reflect on dogs—especially pure-bred dogs—and how they were originally bred for a series of specific purposes—hunting ducks, flushing out foxes on the hunt, herding livestock, or eating vermin and rodents. The American Kennel Club website says Aussie terriers were bred to be "fearless, all-purpose exterminators," specializing in snakes and small mammals, and "eternally

devoted pets when the day's work was done." While rodent hunting might not seem like a higher calling to us, I have seen chipmunk and marmot-chasing dogs who appear to be the happiest of
earth's creatures. Contrast this with humans who spend so many
days casting about without finding a person, an activity, or a cause
that brings a spark to their lives. Yogi Berra was right—"You can
observe a lot by watching." After two years of treading water, I was
thrilled to have my life inspired again, this time by a new passion
for mountain hiking. The joy Emme brought to our experiences
was helping me to see and feel more of that spark every day.

As winter gave way to spring, Emme and I found ourselves
teaming up for hikes with Shan Stuart, a longtime Aspen local
who loves the mountains and loves dogs. In fact, caring for pets
of Aspen families is one of the ways he makes his living, which
works out great for dogs in his care who happen to like the outdoors. Slight of build and a little over fifty years old, he looks
much younger and puts up more hiking and walking miles than
any three people I know combined. It was Shan who put together a
list of fifty "named" hikes for us to try after I shared with him that
I'd like to make my hikes with Emme more challenging.

I hadn't been paying attention to how quickly Emme had
developed her daredevil hiking skills until a day when Pamela and
Tucker, our male Aussie and star show dog, accompanied us on
a hike on Lost Man Trail, a moderately demanding hike that tops
out at an elevation of 12,800 feet. Emme always loved to show off
for other dogs, and this was particularly true when the dog needing to be impressed also happened to live in our home. Where she
might do some modest hopping around to impress one of Shan's
canine hiking guests, she used everything in the bag when the

audience was her housemate. Honestly, I hadn't realized how fast she'd graduated from rock-to-rock dancing to leaping long distances between huge boulders. I'll let Pamela take it from here:

> At one point I saw that there seemed to be just air between two of the rocks she had just jumped, so I walked over to look closer. I nearly fainted. The rocks had about a 1 million–foot drop between them. I started to scold Rick, and he said, "You don't know half of the things she does." That's when I had to tune out. That day was pretty much the end of our hiking as a family.

Emme exhibiting her cleverness, athleticism, and fortitude.

When we got into more serious boulders—twice as big as she was—I became even more aware of her determination and cleverness. When she reached a hard-to-cross stream or rock formation, she would never accept a lift from me but would instead pause and then puzzle out an alternate approach. On many occasions, her new route worked better for me as well.

As to Emme's sense of trail, we know that practically all the information a dog sees and understands comes through his (or her) nose. While not 100 percent perfect, Emme was usually better in leading us down the mountains, rarely hesitating even when physical signs would wear thin or disappear. I wonder if this was because prior hikers in the area might have left clues, such as small, visible disturbances on the trail or traces of smells she can detect more readily by being built closer to the ground and having far superior scent-detection tools. And could the return trip down the mountains be producing fresher scents of people and dogs?[1] There were countless times when I followed Emme down a path that seemed counterintuitive, only to have a cairn or the main trail segment reappear to confirm we were headed in the right direction.

There was another memorable hike during those years when Emme and I were expanding our adventures to higher altitudes—and not just because it took place on my birthday, July 20, 2006. Shan and I had often seen a mountain called Mountain Boy in the distance as we looked to the south from our hikes up around Independence Pass. The parking lot is reachable by way of a narrow road to 12,100 feet. Finding no research online for the best way from where we were to the Mountain Boy summit (13,193 feet), we improvised and invented one.

---

1 For more about the incredible olfactory powers of our four-legged pals, I strongly recommend Alexandra Horowitz's fascinating book *Being a Dog*—a rare combination of serious science, love of dogs, and a writer with a terrific sense of humor. It's a good one.

The plan seemed to take shape when we saw what looked to be a direct path to a ridge that led to the summit. It was steep for sure, but I figured it was still just a slope with small patches of grass and small rocks and pebbles. Not yet skilled at sizing up the best approach on a steep slope to a ridge, I made a rookie mistake and started hiking straight up. Shan knew better and had moved over to the grassier patches that gave his boots a firmer grasp on the mountain. Suddenly, I reached a spot where everything moved, and it felt as though I was standing on loose marbles. The options—continue to ascend, lose traction altogether, and slide down the rocks. Or reverse course, which would also result in a bad slide, given how far I had committed myself onto the slope.

I was stuck. Happy birthday, indeed.

With her four built-in crampons (paws in the role of hiker's spikes) working their magic, Emme stood right at my side, having no trouble herself but clearly concerned about the predicament of her favorite hiking partner. But of course, there was nothing she could do to get me out of this one. Shan called over to me to shimmy laterally toward him where the grass patches were. "Easier said than done," I shouted back. Fortunately, I had hiking poles with me with sharp points, and I began to figure out an exit plan. I shortened them as far as they would go, using them as spikes, and stabbing them into the loose slope to gain purchase. That was the technique I used to slowly move laterally toward Shan, where I was able to gain traction in the firmly rooted small grass pods. We then made our way over to a long patch of snow left over from the winter, still around because it had been shaded by a boulder rib. Finding handholds in the rocks and places to jam our boots between the snow and the rocks, we made it up the snow, Emme flying up but watching me constantly. She and I had ramped up our adventure level—perhaps a little too much—and her body language screamed that she was all in.

Emme and Shan working up the crack between the snow and the rock; Emme was stable even fully on the snowy incline using all fours. The Mountain Boy summit is visible in the far upper left.

Finally, we reached a point where we could see the direct approach to the summit. It was far less taxing to be hiking on a more moderate slope. A man-made pile of rocks and a summit canister awaited us at the top. As I signed in, I felt a feeling of special awe wash over me, and Emme seemed to feel it, too, probably helped along by a sense of relief after a challenging trip. At

13,193 feet, we were higher than either of us had ever been in our lives, at least outside an airplane. Every direction offered views of peaks and valleys that took my breath away on this day that had given us perfect weather.

Instead of taking in the view, Emme was sniffing everywhere. The scrub plants held tufts of off-white fur that had gotten pulled from animals we learned were mountain goats. We looked off in the distance and spotted a large grouping of them at a lower altitude, yet the tufts and Emme's sniffing frenzy proved that they occasionally make it up to the summit. Amazingly, their climbing skills are such that they can navigate ridges steeper than the ones that challenged us. It was exciting seeing them in their native habitat.

After food and water, we headed back down the way we had come up, with Emme devouring her (and my) favorite, turkey-and-Swiss sandwiches, and Shan finishing off his favorite nut mix. The steep snowfield required some real care not to slip and shoot down at high speed into rocks, but there was no other way down. Once again, Emme had no problem. The hiking sticks again came in handy for me, this time in stabilizing the descent. Once we got down to the grassy area, it was an easy trip to the car from there.

That whole day was sensational—combining adventure, discovery of the route, physical challenge, incredible views, and a sense of accomplishment. We had reached the summit and made our names part of the summit canister. No one could ask for a better birthday gift.

When we got into the car, Emme jumped onto her spot on the armrest and just looked triumphant. She looked at me and right then I knew exactly what she was communicating: *Hey, you finally figured it out. This is my purpose. It is what I want to do, and you're going to do it with me.* At that moment I knew we were onto something. That I was sixty-three years old as I became serious about mountain climbing was an issue of concern for my friends more than it was for me. Our experience of reaching the summit of Mountain Boy felt like I'd reached the point in a journey that was only just beginning.

CHAPTER 7

LET'S GET LOST

*Some beautiful paths can't be discovered
without getting lost.*

—Erol Ozan

Rick and Emme reunited, tearfully.

Reaching the summit of Mountain Boy on my sixty-third birthday during the summer of 2006 was one of the most satisfying hikes ever for Emme and me, and it got me wondering what would be next for us. Shan had researched about fifty hikes for us within an hour's drive of Aspen, and throughout the fall, we enjoyed at least a dozen of those outings with our various hiking pals, always trying to explore trails that were compatible with the dogs who would be coming along with us. Emme, of course, was up for whatever came our way, with a preference for excursions that promised the most opportunities for adventure and high places. For her, this meant plenty of interesting scents on and off the trail, as well as a chance to show off her prowess to whatever other dogs might be accompanying us.

Another reason why things were looking up around this time was because my son Brett had decided to live close by. After graduating from NYU's Stern Undergraduate College with a BS degree in Business, Brett had won a competition to spend a year in India working for Mphasis, a call-center outsourcing company. This was after he had taken off a semester of college to live in Ecuador and learn Spanish. When he returned to the United States in mid-2005, I was thrilled when he settled down a few miles from our home, living with his dog Amos in an authentic miner's cabin in downtown Aspen.

After years of scuba diving and skiing together, I looked forward to sharing my new passion for mountain hiking with Brett. If you think I needed to train him, then guess again. Upon settling in Aspen, he accepted a full-time job with the top mountain gear company in the area, Ute Mountaineer, where he embodied the company's stated mission of employing "The people who know and use the gear they sell." A future top finisher in Ironman Triathlons (including Hawaii), Brett is an athlete whose bosses at Ute had encouraged him to embrace the mountains and all other aspects of Colorado's lifestyle. As you might expect, he was a natural, quickly developing high-end, year-round outdoor skills under the tutelage of the area's most skilled technical hikers and elite, high-performance skiers. By the late spring of 2006, Brett could have qualified as a full-fledged mountain guide and had even considered it as a profession. He was that good.

Brett's development practically overnight into an exceptional mountain skier and hiker was an accomplishment that brought me great pride. But based on his first climbing experience on the mountains of Colorado, I am surprised he ever made his way back to them.

That story begins with Pamela's son, Clayton, who has become a second son to me. Five years apart in age, both Clayton and Brett were avid adventurers. But unlike Brett and me, Clayton's inclination is to leap in with minimal instruction or preparation, skipping the part where some people would take time to research, train, and plan. By winging it, he has arrived at outcomes that have been highly entertaining and hilarious, while others have made my head throb.

For instance, Pamela tells the story of Clayton showing her a video of him skydiving, after which she was almost relieved he'd survived the jumps. Everything he was describing seemed to be in the past tense, and her initial reaction was that he'd gotten another wild hobby out of his system without major injuries sustained. *Um,* not really, said Clayton, pointing out that having reached the milestone of fifty jumps, he was now qualified to jump *alone*. I assure you this was *not* what his mother wanted to hear. With Pamela's rational appeals falling on deaf ears, Clayton returned to Florida to successfully carry out five hundred solo jumps from airplanes—before permanently hanging up his jumpsuit.

The first time Brett and Clayton combined forces for an outdoor activity took place on the morning of August 29, 2000, which just happened to be the day on which Pamela and I were to be married. The boys were in town for the ceremony, after which Brett would fly to New York City to begin his first year at NYU.

Over breakfast, I recall Clayton tossing out a suggestion to Brett that went something like, "Let's take a quick ride up to Independence Pass where there's a lot of great rock climbing. We'll be back in plenty of time to get ready for this afternoon." Clayton had taken an intensive thirty-day rock climbing course while visiting his mother in Colorado about four or five years earlier and, after giving up the rocks for whatever was next, had placed his equipment in storage. He added, "I only have gear for one—but we can share." To Brett it must have sounded intriguing: rock climbing on a glorious Colorado morning right before heading off to school. Off they went.

From both accounts, the boys drove the twenty-mile scenic route at 11,300 feet until they spotted a lineup of cars parked on the side of the road right next to a cliff wall. To Clayton, the presence of cars meant they'd found a popular area and as good a spot as any for them to set up shop. As a first step, Clayton decided to set a "top rope," which they did by circumventing the cliff and hiking up the side to the top. He then proceeded to set the safety rope and dangle it over and down the cliff. All good so far. The safest way to experience a Class 5 "technical" climb—which is pretty much a wall with a few places to stick your hands and feet—is to do roughly what they did. First, fasten a rope from the top, then start climbing from the bottom, using the rope as a safety belay (secure rope) in case someone loses his or her grip and falls off the wall.

The first problem they encountered had to do with the calendar —in August 2000, Brett's life skills did not yet involve teaching people how to set up rock climbing equipment. That would not be the case until 2005. With no idea how to use the gear, he found himself deferring to Clayton as the subject-matter expert. But for his part, Clayton was only slightly ahead of Brett, given the five years—and little practice—that had transpired since his intensive month of rock-climbing classes. But his relative status as the more experienced climber meant that Clayton would need to tie Brett into the harness and send him rappelling down the wall first. For those of you not familiar with rappelling, it entails stepping or jumping over a cliff wall and walking down with one's feet pointed into the wall. Jason Stratham does a pretty good job of it in the remake of *The Mechanic*.

As preparations continued, Clayton's rustiness on the rocks began to show. As he struggled to recall the precise knots required to secure Brett into the harness, Clayton turned to reference materials, pulling out his trusty copy of *How to Rock Climb* to refresh his memory. But unfortunately, as he was flipping through the manual in search of knot options, a gust of wind blew the book out of his hands and over the side of the mountain. This was no longer an open-book test. "Don't worry," said Clayton. "I know some decent knots. They should be good enough to get us to the bottom."

Tied into the harness with the best knots Clayton could remember from five years earlier, Brett stepped over the side and began to rappel down toward the bottom. The plan was that once Brett reached the ground, he would untie and release the rope so Clayton could tie himself in and repeat Brett's trip. They would both then begin climbing up, using the secured rope for safety. Makes sense. Easy enough.

Except things didn't go according to plan. Brett rappelled for a few minutes out of Clayton's sight, at least until Clayton heard him shouting up the ridge. The following transcript of their conversation was recently deemed "close enough" by the two participants, who were communicating at a distance from one another of about eighty feet:

Brett: *Hey, Clayton, I'm out of rope.*
Clayton: *Are you at the bottom?*
Brett: *No. I am not at the bottom. I am about fifty feet from the bottom.*
Clayton: *Is the rope stuck on anything?*
Brett: (Pause) *Nope. I can see it clearly all the way up, and it's not stuck on anything.*
Clayton: *Then what's the problem?*
Brett: *It's too short.*
Clayton: *(Silence)*
Brett: *What now Clayton? Well?*
Clayton: *I'm thinking.*

Clayton later claimed he was under the impression that most climbs in the Independence Pass area were seventy-five feet or less and that he had planned accordingly. This meant that when doubled, a standard 150-foot rope would have been long enough to reach the ground. But Clayton had unknowingly selected a

120-foot climb, didn't premeasure the total drop, and the realities of rope math left Brett dangling at a height of forty-five feet, give or take. On the flip side, at least full marks go to Clayton for his decision to take the precautionary step of tying off the bottom of the rope, so it could not pass through the harness. This was likely a life-saver, or at least a serious-fall saver, for Brett. Climbing the eighty feet wasn't a good option either for Brett without additional equipment and more training, both of which he would have in six years—but not today. Both of our guys somehow managed to stay cool even as Brett dangled at forty-five feet, Clayton struggled for solutions, and both had a wedding to attend in three hours.

In a stroke of luck, their ordeal ended safely and happily. Two experienced climbers with plenty of gear were ascending nearby on the same wall and, seeing Brett's predicament, bailed him out by offering their rope and helping him navigate his way to the bottom. It's become a much-retold family story, taking place as it did on the morning of our wedding and characterizing the "Ready, shoot, aim" approach to life that defined Clayton when he was in his mid-twenties. It also says everything you need to know about Brett that, after a close brush with a dangerous situation on the mountain rocks, he would in short order grow into an expert alpinist, a pro-level skier, and an EMT for Aspen's Mountain Ambulance with advanced avalanche certification.

As much as I liked to think that Brett and I err on the side of overpreparation for both our shared and separate adventures, I learned that even the most precise planning still leaves one with thousands of variables, at least on a mountain hike. By researching the inside information on the trails, the distinctive landmarks, and the expected challenges, I figured we had cut the total number of variables in half. Part of the prep is also contingency planning—having plenty of food and water, packing an extra pair of sunglasses, and bringing along a first aid kit and sunscreen. Also, one must always bring a GPS communicator of some kind. And no matter what the forecast says, pack enough warm and waterproof clothes to keep you comfortable in bad weather. A picture-perfect day with a radiant and clear blue sky can turn dark and cold in a hurry during a hike in the Rockies. Watch the weather, and always turn back before lightning strikes. The one sure lesson I have taken away from the mountains: expect the unexpected.

Shan's research helped Emme and me to start exploring several of the bigger "named" hikes around the Aspen area, providing us with new ways to experience the richness of the outdoors in the Rockies. We had our favorite hikes, generally one to three hours in length. It was always Emme and me on these hikes, although Shan and Brett and sometimes Dennis and Dexter would join us when their schedules allowed.

As we explored Shan's list and kept going higher, we often wound up on Independence Pass. Narrow lanes, huge drop-offs, and the sparse installation of guardrails at over 11,000 feet make this a white-knuckle ride for many—but not for Emme. From the parking lot and viewing platform at that altitude, there are several mountains accessible in the range of 13,000 to 13,500 feet. Up we went.

It was on one of these mountains, about 1,000 feet up from the pass, that we "discovered" a rocky overhang at 13,000 feet that I came to call our Zen Hangout. The landmark for it was a vertical stone shaped like a milk container that was visible all the way down to the Independence Pass parking lot. About fifty feet to the right (south) of the milk container and thirty feet down from it is a small shelf on the ridge that faces east and is only accessible through a notch in the ridge wall. The total length of the ledge is about eight feet, and from the ridge wall to the cliff drop-off measures only three feet. I would sit with my legs hanging over the cliff, while Emme sat about a foot from the edge, alternately transfixed on either the heart-stopping views or on whatever I happened to be eating.

The full hike up to the obelisk (vertical rock); the Zen spot is a bit to the right of it and on the other side of that ridge.

Since it wasn't listed in the guidebooks, didn't have a cool name, and did not qualify as a summit, our spot was rarely trafficked. No complaints there. It became our ritual to eat Fig Newtons and turkey sandwiches while we took in the vast panoramas to the southeast. On certain days, I could almost reach out and touch the puffy clouds, some of which floated past below where we were perched. The vista was boundless, and I could see for such a distance that it felt as though I could see into the future. It felt a million miles from a world of texts, emails, deductibles, and co-pays. If we stayed here long enough, my brain finally would relax, and ideas would blow in. As we sat on the edge of a cliff that dropped off forever, not once did I fear Emme would lose her balance or make a dangerous lunge at a rodent too close to the precipice. Remarkably, I cannot recall her barking or interrupting even once during those times, as she also seemed to be meditating and sharing a sense of awe for where we were and what that hallowed place came to mean to us.

Our Zen Hangout didn't simply provide us with a destination; it also gave us the bonus of the uphill hike from the Independence Pass parking lot to reach it. It allowed Emme to renew her acquaintance with marmots, which she has always loved to chase back into their holes for sport, and ptarmigans, which presented a more complicated arsenal of skills when eluding their pursuers. A bird in the grouse family weighing in at a little over a pound, the ptarmigan can both run and fly, bad news for its predators. They take the land option whenever possible because it's easier on their bodies—flying expends too much of the tiny bird's limited stockpile of stored energy. When Emme took off after one as we hiked at 12,500 feet, it looked like Wile E. Coyote chasing the cartoon Roadrunner, with the ptarmigan maintaining a slight but steady lead throughout the entire chase. Emme gamely kept things competitive—right up until the moment when the fleet little bird ran off a cliff, flapped its wings, and began to fly. As surprising as beholding the bird heading airborne was Emme's ability to immediately call on all sixteen of her claws to bring her momentum to a halt just short of disaster. As I recall asking myself at the time, was it part of the ptarmigan's historical DNA to run animals with bad intentions off the edge of steep cliffs? A day in the life of a ptarmigan would make for a lively segment of the BBC series *Planet Earth*.

With dog-human communications having their limits, it's hard to say what Emme took away from that surreal first experience with a ptarmigan. I know that watching the not-so-small bird first run like the wind and then take off and fly certainly grabbed my attention, and it sent me to the internet that evening to learn more. Over time, I think Emme's response was more along the lines of *Boy, was that fun* because she loved a spirited chase and never stopped going all out in pursuit of ptarmigans.

To this day, I am convinced that a ptarmigan figured into an incident that occurred in the late summer that forever changed Emme's (and my) approach to how we would hike together from that day forward. Since it would be just Emme and me that day, I figured the numbers were steering us to our Zen Hangout, which comfortably fit the two of us. With plenty of small animals in the mix, no shortage of terrain challenges, and the absence of a clear trail, the hike threw just enough curveballs and physical demands to make us earn our meditation time in the clouds.

The first part of the climb took us through the willows, which on this mountain were bushes that grow from three to six feet tall and often too dense to force one's way through. Part of the fun was finding the gaps between bushes, much like navigating a maze. Getting past the willows, Emme led the way as we made our way to steeper ground through a rocky approach to the high meadow we knew so well by that time. She continued to lead the way until she was out of sight, and I could no longer see her orange vest. It was about 11:30 AM.

At first, I wasn't concerned because this was such familiar territory for her, as well as for me. But maybe familiarity had become part of the problem, in that she was tending to stray farther away from me each time we went up there. I was also just coming to learn one of the primary lessons of the mountains—that it doesn't take more than a couple of hundred feet (or less) of separation to lose a partner. Also, for those relying on sight, clusters of rock, gullies, ridges, or cliff bands can fool anybody into believing he or she is in territory that feels visually recognizable when it can also be a case of so many areas sharing common geologic features.

When Emme and I had become momentarily separated previously, the solution would be for me to stop and wait, and she would quickly locate me, thanks to dogs' superior senses of smell and hearing. But maybe in this instance I didn't realize in time that she was lost and likely didn't stop soon enough for her to find me. Or perhaps she got distracted—possibly by a ptarmigan—and chased the little bird farther away than usual from our well-established route. Also, where I stood, at about 13,000 feet and 1,000 feet above the tree line, had no trail. I shouted her name for a half-hour, but with winds of 25–30 mph at that altitude, sound was likely getting muffled, which could explain why my calls were not reaching her. By 1 PM, I had been calling her for over an hour and a half. I was getting nervous.

My experience over the years is when dogs and their owners have become separated on a mountain, the dog's instinct is to track downward toward the trailhead on the route the dog knows well from having just ascended it. But I wasn't completely sure of this behavior on that day as I am now. I was certain that Emme knew her way back down to the parking lot, although crossing

State Highway 82 would be a risk, since she had only done that while on a leash. After ninety minutes of hiking all around where I had last seen her, shouting as I went, I decided to hike the mile and a half (1,000 feet in elevation) downhill and back to the parking lot, which would take me about forty-five minutes. It was during the descent that an escalating-but-controlled panic began to course through my brain and heart. I kept in mind that big data statistics favor happy reunions between lost dogs and their owners, but this didn't factor in a unique set of variables at 12,000 feet.

When I arrived at the parking lot, she wasn't there. And no one I engaged down there had seen her. The circumstances weren't exactly like the TV show *48 Hours,* but the idea was the same—the more time that passes without finding her reduces the likelihood that she'll be found. Distraught, I hiked the mile and a half back up the mountain to search for her. My brain was working overtime, but the options were starting to narrow. Of course, I would never leave the area without her, but I was not equipped for an overnight stay at 12,000 feet (at temperatures often below freezing) if it came to that. Mobile phones didn't work on the mountain, and it would require a nineteen-mile drive to Aspen to get cell service. Besides, I was too afraid to leave the area, believing that the moment I decided to drive back into town would be the moment when Emme would come looking for me. During my hikes up and down the mountain, to and from the parking lot, I resolved that there was no way I was leaving—I was going to stay up there all night. If Emme had to brave the overnight cold, then so would I.

It's hard even now to express the depth of my fear, frustration, and helplessness. Not to mention the self-incrimination because in my mind, this one was on me. Adrenaline likely masked that I was exerting myself far beyond my normal limits, but my fears and despair were driving me. What if she was gone for good? Had she been stolen? I was pretty sure there were no coyotes or mountain lions above the tree line, but that was cold comfort. What was Emme thinking at that moment? Surely, she was looking for me as desperately and futilely as I was looking for her. That last thought made me incredibly sad.

What I didn't know is that an amazing story was unfolding back at the parking lot. Emme must have ranged far afield, for whatever reasons. (Took the route of the hike for granted? Got turned around while chasing a ptarmigan?) Unable to locate me, she assumed I would be waiting for her down at the parking lot, which meant crossing State Highway 82, which wasn't heavily trafficked—about five to ten cars per hour—but still a major cause for concern. She did this, according to a couple (who has since become our friends), after which she wandered from group to group in the parking lot, searching for me. Understanding her plight, these thoughtful people lifted her up and noticed she had a tag with her name and a phone number. Unable to call due to no cell service, they saw the quality of her grooming and figured Emme must be from Aspen. Finding another couple in the parking lot who would be heading down to Aspen shortly, they persuaded them to hand Emme over to the Aspen sheriff. Our soon-to-be new friends then went the extra mile and took the second couple's contact info and license plate number, saying they would be calling the sheriff within an hour to verify that the dog had been turned over.

By 4 PM, the sheriff had received Emme and had called Pamela, who immediately sprang into action. She assumed both that I didn't know Emme had been found and that I would not come down from the mountain until I found her. After picking up Emme at the police station, Pamela drove the nineteen miles straight up to the Independence Pass parking lot and waited. It wasn't long after she arrived that I reached the bottom leg of one of my loops to check the parking lot. Identifying Pamela's car, I made a beeline for it and spotted Emme. Without speaking, Pamela opened the passenger door, and Emme jumped out and up into my arms. For a few minutes I completely lost it, overcome with emotion. It felt as though after spending hours in a dark hole and with no way out, someone had thrown me a lifeline. It was the worst of bad dreams from which I had just been awakened. A few minutes later, the thought of it seemed so confusing and almost too horrible to have really happened until Pamela told me the story.

After this incident, Emme's behavior on the mountain trails became both life-changing and hike-changing. She would check far more frequently to make sure she knew where I was. As we took on more serious climbs with younger and faster hikers, she appointed herself as the "connector"—running uphill to spot our colleagues, then running back until I could see her and she could see me. This behavior was enormously helpful as we attempted more difficult peaks because it allowed me to climb with, and stay visually attached to, faster-moving hiking partners. In the higher mountains, the margins of error became further reduced—as little as fifty feet of separation can place you out of sight of your group, in a completely different gully or on another side of a rock rib.

The problem of my keeping up with and preventing separation from faster hikers was solved by Emme's intuition and diligence. There is no question in my mind that it also came from her determination that we would never lose one another on a mountain again.

Emme's desire to climb started when she was very young. This was taken on the Taylor Pass Trail. Taylor Pass was once the main supply route from Buena Vista into the mining camps around Ashcroft, originally known as Castle Forks.

We gave Emme a shot at motherhood, but it was a one-and-done for her. Pictured here are her puppies at eight weeks old.

"Tag, you're it!" Swimming in the pond with the koi fish, which were nearly her size, was Emme's second favorite activity.

Emme was never intimidated by larger dogs, as shown here at dog camp.

Tight-roping a log near camp.

Back in Aspen, all she wanted to do was hike—
and eat my turkey sandwich.

Emme can be seen in the foreground of this photo just before her fearless parting of the bulls.

Taking a load off our feet—and paws—at our Zen spot. La Plata Peak, the fifth-highest summit of the Rocky Mountains, rises prominently in the background.

Snow? No problem! Emme always made the first tracks.

Keeping up with her was not easy.
Here I am, post-holing through the deep snow.

Wherever we went, she went higher.

Emme did whatever it took to get the job done—including balancing on two legs to get up the rocks.

How in the world did she get up there?

Was there any rock formation she couldn't climb?

Our first big summit, Mountain Boy, elevation 13,210 feet.

The views from the summit never fail to inspire awe.
Grizzly Peak, rear center, is the highest thirteener at 13,995 feet.

The wind was pretty fierce at the top of
Electric Pass, elevation 13,485 feet.

The zig-zag route up 14,154-foot Mount Democrat.

Emme always waited for me to catch up
and made sure she was in sight.

The beautiful San Juan Mountain Range, as seen from the summit of Sunshine Peak.

We were happy and relieved to be off the mountain after safely navigating through thunder, lightning, hail, and driving rain.

Enjoying the summit at Mount Bierstadt,
elevation 14,065 feet.

On the way to Mount Antero, upper right.

Emme on the climb up Grays Peak. She was always a
sentinel for me, connecting me to the faster climbers.
Somehow, she found a way up this steep face.

Incredible views from Mount Massive, elevation 14,429 feet.

Summit of Mount Missouri, elevation 14.075 feet, with Laura.

Emme's last climb took us up Mount Sopris,
ablaze in autumn colors.

En route to Mount Sopris, the aspen leaves
glittered down the gullies like rivers of fire.

At age fourteen, Emme was still outpacing her much younger male buddies.

Emme "Lucky Lady"—surely my best friend.

EMME LEVY CRANDALL

JANUARY 31, 2001 TO AUGUST 27, 2015

CHAPTER 8

MOUNT YALE:
OUR FIRST FOURTEENER

It's a round trip. Getting to the top is optional.
Getting down is mandatory.

—Ed Viesturs, *No Shortcuts to the Top*

Coming down off the summit of our
first fourteener, Yale Peak.

Right up until the moment I blacked out and fell forward while gasping for air, Wednesday, September 12, 2007, had been one of the happiest and most satisfying days of my life. It had long been circled on the calendar as the day Emme and I would attempt a climb to the summit of Mount Yale, which would be our first attempt at a mountain summit higher than 14,000 feet in elevation. One of the so-called "fourteeners," Mount Yale forms part of a group of almost-mythic granite peaks that continue to attract an ever-increasing mix of Colorado locals and mountain-climbing enthusiasts from around the world.

When Brett happened to have a day off and was available to make the climb with us, a day already circled on the calendar became even more exciting and meaningful.

From the time I arrived in Colorado back in 2000, it has been difficult to ignore the constant buzz about the "fourteeners." One reason is that they rise above our part of the country the way the Empire State Building, the Chrysler Building, and neighboring skyscrapers tower above New York City. Another compelling reason for the notoriety is that the fourteeners are as high as one can climb above sea level in the contiguous United States. Want to bag a peak that is 15,000 feet or higher? That will require a trip to Alaska. In fact, there are only four states with mountain peaks over 14,000 feet—Colorado, Alaska, California, and Washington. (Utah's King's Peak falls a long home run short at 13,534 feet.)

Due to our work commitments, Brett and I skipped the overnight motel near the trailhead, which turned the outing into a day trip. The upside of leaving home in the 4 AM predawn darkness was being treated to a two-hour light show through my windshield for which Colorado might think about charging admission to fund the state treasury. The billions of stars visible on the ride from Aspen over Independence Pass and into Buena Vista remind me of a high-tech version of the hokey Laserium shows that took the country's planetariums by storm during the 1970s. All that was missing were the sweet-smelling herbs, an inexpensive 2-D laser machine, and a sound system playing Pink Floyd at volume 11.

Emme assumed her usual surfing position on the console of the 4Runner, her eyes always on the road, poised to alert the driver when he or she has missed a turn. After driving hundreds of hours on Highway 82 over Independence Pass to various hiking destinations, I have noticed she no longer simply reacts to the hairpin turns—she's begun to anticipate them. Pamela's theory about Emme's console surfing—a performance she pulls off without seatbelts, straps, buckles, or deep claw marks into the upholstery—is that it's a regimen of pre-hike balancing exercises so that she is ready hit the trail running. As I would always do on Highway 82, I wondered if Emme also silently questioned the wisdom of so few guardrails and the frequent narrowing of lanes on the highest paved mountain pass (12,095 feet) in North America.

Today's hike to the summit of Mount Yale will be my first fourteener but not Brett's, not by a long shot. Now twenty-five years old and still working at Ute Mountaineer, he has gained acknowledgment as one of the area's competent technical mountain climbers after less than two years of living in Aspen. He learned the ropes (sorry) from the best climbers in the Aspen area and with the full support of his outdoor-minded employer by way of gear, encouragement, and time off. It also didn't hurt that he came to the mountains in top physical shape and has always been a quick study when learning new skills throughout his life.

One of the main reasons I found myself on the verge of attempting a Colorado fourteener at the age of sixty-four was because I was either pushed or pulled into mountain climbing by Emme, my strong-willed Aussie terrier. I continued to marvel at the pure joy she displayed whenever I picked up her orange hiking vest in advance of one of our almost-daily adventures on the mountain trails. "Someday," I told myself back when Emme was years younger, "I want to be as happy about *anything* as Emme is about hiking." Several years later, as the Mount Yale hike drew nearer, my enthusiasm about climbing mountains was slowly building to Emme-like levels.

This won't be the first hike together for Brett and me; there have probably been dozens of medium-altitude hikes for us since he returned from India to live in Aspen a couple of years earlier. For me, one of the highlights of engaging in outdoor activities with Brett after so many years was less about the deep conversations and more about the shorthand with which we communicated. As the old aphorism goes, sometimes less is more. By the time we passed Buena Vista and reached Cottonwood Pass, we had exchanged paragraphs of information with raised eyebrows, head nods, and several monosyllabic grunts. That was about all we had in us at that early hour of the morning.

When we arrived at the Denny Creek trailhead (9,900 feet) for Mount Yale just before 6 AM, it was still dark but wouldn't be for long. The sunrise soon replaced the stars with a brilliant purple-pink sky as we made final preparations for the climb. Despite trailhead temperatures in the low forties, Brett and I had both decided on shorts with four layers of shirts and tops, expecting midday highs in the mid-sixties that would feel even warmer as we hiked.

Mount Yale's approach is just under five miles and 4,300 feet of elevation, 3,900 feet of which takes place over the first three and a half miles. This hike, sections of it anyway, will require rigorous climbing, akin to about 400 flights of stairs. (By comparison, reaching the Empire State Building Observation Deck, requires 86 flights of stairs and offers no chance of cavorting with marmots.) And with the final 250 to 300 feet of the route on what is called the summit cone to Yale's peak reaching the category of "Class 2 Difficult," our research told us to prepare for a demanding slog on a surface of small rocks to reach the summit. With those numbers, Mount Yale would serve as an objective yardstick for my improved climbing skills.

A little history on the naming of Mount Yale—the tradition of naming mountain peaks after famous colleges began in 1869 when four members of the first graduating class of the Harvard School of Mining and Practical Geology named a 14,420-foot peak after their institution. The same group then named the adjacent peak Mount Yale in honor of their professor, Josiah Whitney, who led the expedition.

As Brett and I generously applied sunscreen in the quiet darkness before our climb, a precaution we repeated three or four times during the hike, I could feel tension begin to tighten across my chest. It arrived with a surge of adrenaline that made me anxious to burst from the blocks like an Olympic sprinter. There was something unique and almost consequential about taking on a fourteener, especially one with "difficult stretch" built into its bio. The peak of Mount Twining is a rounding error from being a fourteener, yet our having sat atop its 13,711-foot summit a couple of months ago offered me practically no confidence boost at that moment. It felt like the wide chasm between playing minor league baseball and being called up to the big leagues. Reaching the summit of a fourteener is a big-league hike.

Amid this range of emotions on the trailhead, I drew on the words of Denver author Mark Obmascik, who wrote a book about his experiences in bagging Colorado's fourteeners. Referring to the Collegiate Peaks (of which Mount Yale is one), he wrote: "They're hikes. If you have sturdy legs and willing lungs, and a pretty strong heart, you can get up these peaks." My hope was that Obmascik had factored sixty-four-year-old hikers into the mix when he made his assessment.

Today's fourth hiker is a fifty-five-pound two-year-old with a long nose. With those dimensions he would be the talk of preschool if he weren't a dog. I'm referring to Brett's mostly black mixed-breed Amos, who is a welcome guest on today's expedition. Friendly but never cloying, Amos combined a serene temperament with well-above-average stamina and superior hiking skills—he had already become an Aspenite by hiking with Brett and with anyone else in the area who wanted a dog companion. Friends who lived nearby fell over themselves to dog-sit for low-key, friendly, and low-maintenance Amos when Brett was out of town. And if those credentials weren't enough, Amos and Emme were the best of pals and full-time partners in crime on mountain trails.

There was no starter's gun as we began our Mount Yale expedition, although one of us probably muttered, "Let's go." Things

Amos on Mount Yale.

got underway by following the Denny Creek Trail north through a thick forest of tall aspens and mixed conifers. If Colorado had a "state smell" to go along with its state flower (the columbine) and state song ("Where the Columbines Grow"), it would be the unmistakable bouquet of pines and firs, similar to what greeted us at the early stages of this trail.

About a mile on the trail brought us to Denny Creek, the first of several times our path would cross this running stream during today's round trip. It presented an opportunity for Emme to show off her nifty dance steps for an audience, as she once again gave her best Gene Kelly impersonation across the extended logs. Back in doggie camp it had been fascinating to watch Emme demonstrate for Cooper the precise footwork needed to navigate makeshift stream crossings. She seemed to understand, however, that there would be no impressing Amos who, with a technique consistent with his extensive alpine experience, plowed ahead without fanfare or hesitation. Seen it, done that.

It helped that the narrow Mount Yale trail was clearly marked with a right-turn sign when, as our research had pointed out, we came to what would have been a confusing fork in the road. Glimpses through the trees suggested a sky in a rich shade of blue other American states can only dream about, a sight we'll be able to enjoy to a greater extent once we hike above the tree line. That we are two-and-a-half miles (and climbing) above sea level translates to less atmosphere (air, humidity, dust, particulates) above us in the troposphere than in, say, Ann Arbor. Thin air also holds less moisture, resulting in less of the high-altitude condensation that adds a white or light component to the sky's natural deep-blue color. This was the science and the conditions that made possible the magnificent Colorado blue sky, particularly impressive when viewed at high altitudes.

These longer and higher-altitude climbs provided me with ample time to get inside my own head, especially after Emme and I began setting our sights on higher summits. Emme and I had spent the six weeks or so leading up to Yale acclimatizing ourselves at higher elevations to prepare for the thin air and lower air pressure at 14,000 feet. In higher elevations as the air became noticeably thinner, I made it priority one to concentrate on my breathing, often at the expense of making small talk with climbing companions.

By my count, we were passed by only two other pairs of hikers on today's ascent. Back when I read that over 30 percent of all hikes of fourteeners take place on Saturdays, it was an easy decision to concede Saturdays—and often Sundays—on the more popular trails to the weekend warriors who needed to climb on weekends. In addition to larger crowds and crowded trails, weekends also tended to bring out a higher percentage of hikers focused on the summit but often ill-prepared in terms of equipment, supplies, advance research, and physical conditioning.

As we settled into the first significant uphill segment of the Mount Yale trail, I could sense my foot speed dropping noticeably, and I caught Brett throttling down to match my pace. Although the hike must have seemed more like a crawl to him, he never mentioned it, nor did he allow himself to get more than fifty feet in front of me at any time. It was a small moment to savor—a nod to his old man carried out in Brett's typical understated way. I felt deeply grateful at that moment for Brett's quiet way of going about things and for the opportunity to share so many wonderful adventures with him over the years.

The only astronaut to fly Mercury, Gemini, and Apollo missions for NASA, the great Wally Schirra, once shared a moving thought about sons: "You don't raise heroes; you raise sons. And if you treat them like sons, they'll turn out to be heroes, even if it's just in your own eyes."

My mind began to wander further off the trail, as I realized the date was September 12. It was six years and one day ago that I spent several hours frantically trying to locate Brett in downtown New York City, where he was attending college. As I did during those uncertain hours of 9/11, I revisited the wacky, complicated thoughts that swirled around in my head on the day Brett was born in 1982.

From as far back as I could recall, I cherished the relationship with my dad. When I got married back in Michigan, I looked forward to a day when I would be able to pass along to my son the love and support my own father had graciously bestowed on me. But on the day Brett was born, rather than imagining our first fishing trip or a game of catch in the backyard, I became stuck on the lyrics to Harry Chapin's "Cats in the Cradle." It was a popular song from those days about how kids gradually and inevitably separate from and discard their parents as they become young adults. What would be the use, I asked myself, of attempting to forge a connection with a son if every parent-child relationship is doomed to fade into one obligatory monthly phone call?

Two and a half miles into the sky and twenty-five years later, I can appreciate how crazy I was to be preparing for a disappearing relationship with a son who was not yet a day old. It also might explain why Brett could swim at the age of four months, ski proficiently at four years, and join me as a certified scuba diver when he was thirteen. It sounds now as though I'd gone through a time when I needed to be needed, training a full-time outdoors sidekick to make myself indispensable. Recently, I joked to a pal, "I chose to teach him skiing and scuba diving because I knew he'd need me for a while just to afford them." The truth is, that it wasn't a joke.

Brett and I worked out fine. We have shared countless outdoor adventures, hundreds of meals, thousands of laughs, and the occasional fork in the road that didn't have a clear trail sign. But if any of our phone calls were obligatory, I certainly don't recall them. All these years down the road, and here we were—hiking into the clouds on a glorious Friday afternoon. And along for the ride were two true friends, Amos and Emme.

Speaking of the dogs, they kept themselves occupied for a solid ninety minutes, although I cannot be more specific than this. From what I gathered, they stayed busy categorizing scents, investigating small animals, following more scents, and accompanying each other off-trail for short nature walks. The dogs had intuitive senses of timing that had them back on the path about ten seconds before we'd have officially marked them with charged absences. I made a note to audit their time cards at the end of the hike to determine exactly how they spent their time.

One activity that was mandated and nonnegotiable on these hikes was drinking plenty of water—and that applied to all four of us. A tube ran from the three-liter water bladder in my pack, running over my shoulder and hanging down the front of my shirt. I brought a red plastic cup connected with a carabiner to my pack strap for Emme. Brett had a similar water system for Amos, and we diligently hydrated all four of us at hourly intervals on the ascent, with the dogs drinking from cups. The intervals could be slightly lengthened on the descent and in cooler or overcast weather. Drinking at intervals wasn't important only for the dogs, it is crucial for two-legged hikers, as well. Thirst becomes a less reliable indicator when a person approaches the age of fifty, so it was essential for the seniors on this hike—that would be me—to set water-break intervals that were based on time, temperature, and level of exertion. Once you feel dehydrated, you are already too far gone to rehydrate quickly simply by guzzling water.

Although the trail of Mount Yale was clearly defined, Emme believed that her job description included keeping everyone in the hiking party connected and on the correct path. In keeping us on the straight and narrow, she likely confirmed our group's direction by sight—she had been on hundreds of trails by this time—and by the smells of the hikers who had already gone up the mountain that morning. But shortly after we crossed Denny Gulch on a log bridge at about 11,000 feet, Emme stopped in her tracks as she heard the *chep, chep, chep* of the whistle pig—the marmot— identified by its badger-like dark brown furry appearance and size, minus the tail. Never one to pass up the thrill of a marmot chase, Emme uncharacteristically decided to skip this one, perhaps sensing that we were in the middle of serious business—a fourteener. And, for her papa, a difficult hike.

When we got above the timber line at 12,000 feet, we began to see more of the hardy animals that lived full-time on the tops of these mountains—the pika, several other species of marmot, and Emme's nemesis, the ptarmigan. It was at this time that I began to feel considerably more lightheaded and unsteady. The air had continued to become thinner, and I wondered how much more altitude I could safely handle. It was of little consolation that my three hiking partners were breathing as though on a Sunday stroll down Main Street.

After covering more ground we could see the summit, now probably a half-mile away as the ptarmigan flies. Less good news— there was still another mile and a half and 300 feet of elevation to cover, all on rough terrain and between boulders on a trail that was now marked only by rock cairns. And though not yet ready for a standing eight-count, I had hit a threshold best described by a boxing announcer as "wobbly."

This is the point in the hike at which Emme took over.

When the defined trail disappeared, she ran well out ahead of us, obviously deeming it her mission to lead us the rest of the way to the top. First, we hit a few steep switchbacks, after which Emme took the approach of hopscotching between boulders, some of

which were larger than she was. Had members of the Flying Wal-
lendas been mixed into her Australian terrier breeding program?
How and where could she possibly have learned these high-wire
skills? Even more amazing is that when I later checked the pads
of her paws for signs of scratches and other injuries she might
have sustained on the sharp rocks, there were none. She was land-
ing her jumps perfectly, as though performing for a panel of dog-
jumping judges.

After slogging and scrambling through the final 250 feet of
large boulders that comprised the "Class 2-Difficult" part of the
Mount Yale summit cone, we made it. Brett, Amos, Emme, and I celebrated at the summit over a gourmet lunch of turkey-and-Swiss
sandwiches and water. A blazing midday sun and nearly cloud-
less sky ensured that the 360-degree panorama was stunning,
with picture-postcard views of the fourteeners Mount Princeton
to the south and Pike's Peak to the east. It was thirty minutes at the
top of Pike's Peak in 1893 that inspired Wellesley College English
teacher Katharine Lee Bates to write a poem about majestic purple
mountains that became the lyrics to "America the Beautiful." But
because my "senior shuffle" pace has resulted in a nearly six-hour
ascent, our foursome must now race the elements—both the late-
summer darkness and the random afternoon thunderstorms on the
mountains back to the trailhead. Our victory lap at the summit was
limited to fifteen minutes—not even enough time to write a poem.

As strange as it sounds, both Emme and I were especially
vigilant about our hiking sticks getting stolen while resting at
the summit. It's no joke. Earlier this year, Emme spotted a stealth
thief—okay, a marmot—swiping a hiking pole at 13,500 feet. The
payoff for the pint-sized pilferers is all about the salt sweat on the

Marmot aiming to steal the hiking sticks.

handles, not in plundering the pole as a hiking accessory. Fortunately, Emme lives on 24/7 marmot alert, which resulted in her catching the criminal in the act and producing her deep bass bark-growl that scared the varmint back into its hole in the boulder field.

After making it down past the rocky cone leading from the summit, I was still fired up because Emme and I were on the board—we had bagged a fourteener. The lingering shot of adrenaline and high emotion sent my policy of limiting conversation out the window. The excitement of climbing to 14,199 feet had made me talkative. Despite feeling the effects of both the thin air and a general heaviness in my legs, I spent fifteen or twenty minutes excitedly blabbering—first to Brett, then to the dogs, and finally to the surrounding mountains—about how great it felt to have finally hiked a fourteener and how perfect it was to have shared the experience with all of them.

Emme in the lead on the way down, as always.

We made decent time in getting within eyesight of the tree line below and with it, the reappearance of the well-marked trail in the distance and the start of the pine trees, at first in miniature size and then a full size smaller than that. It was here that Brett, who had patiently endured my glacial hiking pace on the way up, asked if he and Amos might move things along at a faster clip and try to fit in a stretch of real exercise. They would meet us at the trailhead, he said. It sounded like a perfectly fine plan—the trail was straight-forward, the weather looked clear, and heading downhill, while sometimes more taxing on the knees and ankles, always took less time than the trip to the top. All good here.

Brett and Amos. Brett was happy Amos made it down the rocky Yale summit cone with no foot injuries. It was Amos's first fourteener as well as Emme's.

But after seven hours of climbing, the hike had become more labored than expected. And within fifteen minutes of Brett's depar-ture, I suddenly found myself in full-panic mode—struggling to breathe, with the sensation that my lungs, quads, and head were separately on fire and about to explode. Feeling oxygen-deprived was the most serious of these afflictions because the natural response is to desperately fight harder for each breath, which com-pounds the situation. More oxygen would get into my bloodstream

as I descended to lower altitudes and higher atmospheric pressure,
I reassured myself, but there would be no perceptible improvement anytime soon. The burning in my quads only worsened and
my hips started to ache, and I found myself leaning on my hiking
sticks more than I should. Realistically, I would need to cover at
least a couple of miles on the descent before the increase in air
pressure would kick in enough to help me out of this.

In the middle of the developing crisis I experienced a painful
fall forward, after which I became increasingly more stressed and
unstable. Still needing to cover almost two miles in order to reach
the parking lot at the Denny Creek trailhead, I suddenly feared
that I might not be able to hike out of this. Even if Brett came
looking for me, how would we then get down from the mountain?
I also recalled telling myself that I would never allow myself to be
in such a precarious and life-threatening situation ever again. I
prayed for a helicopter. Or a Saint Bernard.

I had seen several mountain rescues since I'd begun hiking
and had reached two conclusions. The men and women who exe-
cuted helicopter evacuations, often without being able to land the
chopper, were among the most skilled, dedicated, and brave individuals I have ever seen in action anywhere. And my primary goal
on every hike was never be *that* guy—the person whose hiking
accident requires these fearless people to fly into danger and put
their lives and limbs on the line.

Where were all the other hikers when you needed them? As
my lungs burned and my legs wobbled, I did some analysis: 7,000
hikers on Mount Yale over five months. There should be about
forty-seven hikers today, less Brett and me. Allowing that this was
a weekday, there should be thirty people up here today. But given

the urgency of getting off the highest mountains before the after-noon storms come in, most of today's hikers were likely in their cars by 3 PM, or they were relaxing their muscles in the nearby Mount Princeton Hot Springs. The bottom line—I could not expect to be saved by the cavalry.

It was then I recalled the words of George Steinbrenner, of all people. The fiery, controversial owner of the Yankees spent much of his adult life filling the air with military-style quotes he hoped would catch on and adorn the walls of football locker rooms across the country. "Winning is more important than breathing," he once proclaimed to a gaggle of reporters at a spring training press conference. But within seconds he paused and decided to walk it back—"Well, breathing first. Winning next." The Boss had that one right.

Out of desperation, I did the opposite of a Hail Mary pass by employing a strategy I have used over the course of my busi-ness life—breaking down large, daunting tasks into smaller, more manageable, bite-sized pieces. Still needing to rest thirty seconds for every thirty seconds I walked, I decided I would try to cover ground a hundred feet at a time, rambling from tree to tree for balance and then taking as long as I needed to rest. This was tree-hugging taken to an extreme. It would take fifty-two such efforts to advance a mile. The short-term goal was to put one foot in front of the other, even if progress was measured in feet and not miles. I also reminded myself that once I got to the car, I could relax, and Brett could drive us out.

The tree-to-tree strategy resulted in slow-but-sure advance-ment, with Emme making certain that I remained on the trail every step of the way. In addition to calmly reacting to a dangerous situation, she again seemed to understand that this was no time for us to veer off course or for her to be distracted by animals. Locked into the scent of the hikers who had already completed today's round trips, or possibly Amos's lingering scents, she became singularly focused for the duration of what felt to me like the descent that would never end.

By the time Emme and I made it down to the trailhead, over two hours had passed since Brett and Amos left us at the tree line. Our arrival was a relief to Brett, who said he was minutes away from heading back up the trail to take my pack and ease my way.

It had been a rewarding but harrowing nine-hour day on Mount Yale. On the quiet drive home from Mount Yale that night, Brett didn't ask a lot of questions. I filled him in on the basics, saving the unpleasant details for another day. But he could do the math on the two hours it took for me to descend the final few miles. He knew things had become a strain up there.

If Emme and I were going to continue our adventures, then it was decision time. I had watched late-career pro athletes make these decisions since I followed sports as a kid. At some point, everyone must face the limitations of an aging body. In my case, do I scale back, or do I find a less physically demanding activity than mountain climbing? Or is there an attainable level of fitness at my age that would allow me to meet a goal of taking on the fourteeners?

After an hour or so on the road, Brett broke the silence by suggesting that it was possible to turn back the clock, gently adding that it would require rigorous winter training and moderate weight loss. I might have nodded, but all I remember about that ride is being completely drained, both physically and emotionally.

The euphoria of making the summit of Emme's and my first four-teener was tempered by as scary an event of respiratory distress and the worst location for it imaginable. Sure, it's drama—but it's the wrong kind of drama. The words "I don't know if I'm going to make it" can never again be something I say to myself on a mountain trail.

When the dust had settled about a week later, Brett and I had a phone conversation that went something like this:

Me: *So, you mentioned I need to get in better shape?*
Brett: *Yep.*
Me: *So how much better shape?*
Brett: *Much better shape.*
Me: *Put a number on it.*
Brett: *2x.*
Me: *How am I supposed to get in twice as good shape? How do you even measure that?*
Brett: *You'll know.*
Me: *I need to go now.*

My weight of about 195–200 pounds was okay for my 6'1" frame. My size and fitness had served me more than adequately up to that point—I'd been able to scuba dive all over the world, ski on advanced slopes, and walk miles around Ann Arbor without any difficulty. But I had never asked my lungs and legs to climb 14,000-foot mountain peaks until Mount Yale. And I had never been sixty-four years old until two months prior to that hike. My fitness needed to dramatically improve.

The emergency on Mount Yale was an unmistakable wake-up call that I needed to improve my game if I expected to take on those higher altitudes and even more difficult trails. The harsh reality was that regardless of how mountains are officially classified for difficulty, I should not find comfort when ratings and reviews designate a trail as "easy." They might be easier than the trails labeled difficult—which can be downright dangerous—and even an easy trail can become difficult under certain circumstances, such as inclement weather. Moreover, sixty-five years old might be the new fifty, but I also knew that there would never be an "easy" fourteener for someone who has been offered AARP discounts for as long as I have. I would have to earn each fourteener summit from here on.

If I had any hopes of experiencing any of the remaining fifty-seven fourteeners with Emme—*and if it is truly my life's passion to improve as a climber and to learn from each hike*—then Brett was right; I had no choice. Mountain climbing would not work as a life passion unless I could raise my fitness levels and improve my overall health and skill.

CHAPTER 9

SMALL DOG MEETS FOUR TALL PEAKS

*"My father considered a
walk among the mountains as the
equivalent of churchgoing."*

—Aldous Huxley

*Article in the Aspen Times about Emme's summiting
four fourteeners in one day for fun and a fund-raiser.
The photo is of Emme at the fourth summit, Mount Bross.*

I entered the fall of 2007 and winter of 2008 determined not to accept my physical condition made apparent on Yale. Despite the challenges, I loved the physicality, the beauty, the companionship with my son and my dog, and so I resolved that physical preparedness for hiking mountains was within my control. While I could not turn back the calendar or hit a pause button on the passage of years, I was certain I could improve my overall conditioning. Since arriving in Colorado, I had celebrated seven birthdays, but even now I felt ten years younger. If you don't believe age is just a number, consider these numbers—the man who fifty-three years ago wrote "When I'm Sixty-Four," the incredible Paul McCartney, is seventy-seven years old and still performing three-hour concerts in stadiums around the world.

Convinced that what had happened on Mount Yale was just another of life's tests and not a message from the mountain gods to find a different hobby, I resolved to push my fitness into new territory. Rather than retreating, I wanted to keep taking on the fourteeners. This was a whole new category of adventures, with each mountain presenting its own unique challenge for which I would need fitness, new skills, and some friends with a like passion. I already had friend number one in Emme.

Nevertheless, my exuberance needed to be tempered with the reality that the conditioning and recovery time necessary to take on the challenges of hiking the fourteeners enjoyably and without injury would be longer than it would have had I started down this path a decade or so earlier. Still, that made it more of an enticement to me, and I threw myself into it with dogged determination—perhaps inspired by my four-legged hiking companion. I decided to formalize winter and spring daily conditioning. This meant mogul and uphill skiing, aerobics, and strength building until April, followed by "spring training" hikes up lesser mountains as the snow melted and the ski trails became available. My best (and only) chance to keep up with Emme and my younger climbing partners was to whip myself into top shape by the time the summer hiking season arrived.

One of the positive developments of the winter months was finding an instructor who specialized in helping older people to ski moguls in a way that reduces wear-and-tear on our more "experienced" joints and muscles. John Clendenin, former two-time World Freestyle Champion whom some have called the best ski instructor in the world, offers a camp and private lessons employing a style of skiing that enables taking on steeper slopes with moguls but doing so at a slow and controlled speed—the same approach I take to climbing fourteeners during the summer months. It wasn't long before I preferred skiing the bumps instead of the groomed slopes, feeling noticeable cardiovascular benefits even at my deliberate pace.

While the time on the slopes enhanced my overall fitness, skiing doesn't prepare one for climbing. Different leg muscles are involved in each. As I have heard more than one mountain climber point out, skiing down is not the same as hiking up. But what became obvious was that I was now treating ski season as my winter gym. In a few short years, I had gone from receiving a pin for a hundred days of skiing in one winter—a sport I liked—to counting the days until I climbed my next fourteener—an activity that I not only liked but that I aspired to turn into a new life's passion.

Don't laugh—in a town teeming with visitors drawn to Aspen's fifty bars and sizzling après ski nightlife, the highlight of the winter months for me had come to be the time I got to spend in the snow with my Australian terrier. Now able to navigate in fresh snowfalls of ten inches or more as she became more muscular, Emme still insisted on making the first tracks in fresh snow as she led the way up Sunnyside Trail, which was located adjacent to our new home in Aspen. We had, as I recall, between three and five other dogs at the time, including some that Pamela had rescued from being euthanized at a "kill shelter" near a dog show she had attended. While they would tentatively follow only after I had flattened out a makeshift trail with my snowshoes, Emme continued being the lead by hopping out ahead like a bunny for the duration of the hikes, which often lasted an hour or more. She could be sidetracked when she picked up the scents of deer or foxes, but this never lasted for more than a few seconds.

When wet snow began to accumulate in balls on her paws and stomach, she would stop to bite them off so that she could continue to get altitude on her leaps. Propelling herself along in this way had to be exhausting for her, but the only signs of fatigue she'd display would be lying down to rest when she got back to the car or the house—never on the trail. Whether it was making new tracks or hiking established trails with packed snow, Emme and I managed to maintain a winter schedule of completing at least four or five trail walks per week, skipping days only when it was too cold or when I was out of town for work meetings. The new MSR Lightning Ascent Snowshoes had aggressive crampons that allowed me a far

Emme plowing her own first tracks in deep snow.

better grip on the higher trails. I could tell just by the improvement in my daily breathing during all forms of exercise that my stamina was steadily improving.

My packed winter schedule of mogul skiing, snow hikes, and gym work contrasted sharply with how I spent my days in the early 2000s—sitting at the computer and losing myself in spreadsheets and data analysis. My life had reset and refocused on climbing the highest mountains in North America with my friends and my amazing dog. Now lighter between my ears as well as on my feet, I spent days imagining the possible, rather than dwelling on old age, mortality, and the rearview mirror.

To ramp up preparation beyond the winter training, Emme and I added the smallest of Aspen's mountains, Tiehack, to our hiking agenda after skiing had shut down for the year in early April. The word *tiehack* pays tribute to the men who cut and shaped wood from lodgepole pines (that sometimes reach eighteen inches in diameter) into the 8.5-foot railroad ties that helped build the Denver, South Park, and Pacific Railroads in Colorado.

Don't let the "smallest mountain" moniker in reference to Tiehack fool you—the hike, whether taken in the winter or summer, is also described as "quad searing." Tiehack's East Peak has turned into a winter test of endurance for diehard locals determined to hike (with spikes) or ski uphill under their own power, called "skinning." Even post-winter, Tiehack is a steep climb that goes from 8,000 feet to 9,700 feet in a hurry, particularly when Emme and I choose to skip the switch-backed road and hike straight up the slope directly to the top.

With the clock ticking on the summer season, Emme and I climbed Tiehack every other day until it was late May, by which time we had completed twenty-five hikes in fifty days. This brought us to the Thursday before Memorial Day, the annual date for the reopening of the gates that led to Independence Pass on the Continental Divide. Providing us with any number of hikes we enjoyed immensely, Independence Pass featured two special climbs that reached summits of over 13,000 feet, an ideal altitude to acclimatize us for other high thirteeners we'd hike in June and the early part of the summer.

It is essential for hikers to acclimatize because the body needs to adapt to the lower air pressure that exists at high altitudes. For example, while air at all altitudes contains 20.9 percent oxygen, the combination of high altitude and lower air pressure makes it feel as though the percentage of oxygen in that air is also lower.

The air at 14,000 feet has an effective oxygen level of just 12.3 percent, a decrease of 41 percent from how air feels at sea level. The effect ranges from inhaling and feeling like little oxygen is coming in to early symptoms of altitude sickness. They are such things as blue lips, gasping, severe headaches, dizziness, and disorientation. It can create a sense of panic when inhaling seems to provide no oxygen; something went into your lungs, but you are still gasping. There is a strong argument to be made for visitors scheduling a minimum number of days to acclimatize after arriving in Colorado and, when possible, pushing higher-altitude climbs out toward the end of one's stay.

June arrived, and Emme once again surfed the console of the 4Runner and stared out the windshield as we drove the twenty jaw-dropping—and guardrail-challenged—miles on State Highway 82, climbing from Aspen's 8,000 feet elevation to the pass at 12,100 feet. I could sense from her excited demeanor that Emme certainly knew where we were heading. In her mind, Independence Pass was the gateway to the Promised Land. We had been hiking these trails for several years as either the main event or as a prelude to the summer hikes, and, if it is possible, Emme seemed to be even more excited than usual to be on her way to a hiking adventure on this glorious late May morning in the Rocky Mountains. Independence Pass is the highest paved pass in North America, with views so spectacular that they still cause this grizzled local to lose himself in amazement.

We marked the end of spring training by hiking Twining Peak, a low-key thirteener that checks important boxes for both of us. It offers the most artistic rock formations and the early miniaturized high-mountain flowers for me, and it provides occasional wildlife, especially marmots and ptarmigans, for Emme. The unhurried pace at which we traveled left the time we like to smell the roses—or in our case, the hardy alpine buttercup. Resembling a gold boutonniere, this miracle of a flower tracks the sun as it crosses the sky and absorbs radiation, allowing it to survive in colder weather by melting the snow that gathers around it. After learning the backstory on alpine buttercups, I was always on high alert for them, whether they are bending toward the sun in the summer or finding a way to peek out from under the fallen snow during the winter months.

After six stunning climbs of 13,000 feet or higher from Independence Pass, hikes that expanded our lungs and filled our senses, Emme and I were ready for whatever the remainder of the summer would throw at us, ideally on the rare days when the monsoons of July and August are absent from mountain weather forecasts. It turned out that the summer had plenty in store for us, and a quick trip to the archives of the *Aspen Times* helps us revisit the heady excitement of those weeks and days leading to a hike on September 6, 2008. Our hike made the newspapers because, after not having hiked a fourteener with Emme since she steered me down from Mount Yale in 2007, we would be hiking four fourteeners. And we would be climbing all of them for charity—*in one day*.

Before taking on the four peaks, I wanted to put a low-stress fourteener under my belt under the safest possible circumstances, I called Brett and asked to impose on his schedule with a father-son hike, no dogs. He was busy at that time with his job at Ute Mountaineer, as well as with difficult, technical climbs he was able to set up for his days off. The other scheduling complication for us was the July–August monsoon season, which brings dangerous thunderstorms and torrential, rocksliding rains to the mountains. It took a couple of weeks, but we finally found a day in mid-August that combined a low chance of mountain storms and both of us available to hike. We chose Uncompahgre Peak in the western part of the state, Colorado's sixth-highest mountain located in the San Juans, a 7.5-mile hike that offered a 2,800-foot elevation gain.

The significance of the Uncompahgre Peak hike, in addition to spending a full day on a new fourteener with Brett, was that I felt strong throughout the day, from start to finish. Although hikes where I struggled were the exception, I could sometimes lose my fastball and become fatigued at various points on a trail. But not on this day. The consistency of my stamina on Uncompahgre led me to immediately begin planning the next adventure with Emme. It must have been on my mind that we hadn't bagged a fourteener together since Mount Yale, which had been her first and only, when I came across a compelling challenge on a mountain climbing website—that it was possible to climb to the summit of four fourteeners over the course of one hike. Mount Democrat, Mount Cameron, Mount Lincoln, and Mount Bross shared a saddle, and it was possible to reach all four summits in one 7.5-mile hike that formed a loop, which meant no re-summits in order to descend. The day's total hiking elevation would be about 3,700 feet.

In just two phone calls, I assembled our entire team of four. Laura Welch was a go before I'd even mentioned the date or fully described what the day would entail. In her early fifties at that time, Laura had excellent balance and easily handled the rocky portions of trails. Diana Peckham was not a regular member of our group but made a case with her enthusiasm for this specific hike.

Diana's husband, Rick Peckham, was our fourth team member and the ringer of our group. Rick was approaching his mid-fifties but kept his fitness up at all times. Quiet and unassuming, he is a retired Air Force Special Operations Command Pararescueman (PJ for short). As a climber, he reached the 20,310-foot summit of Alaska's Denali (formerly Mount McKinley) twice as part of his military training and was credited with saving fifty-seven lives in the dozens of his civilian and military missions. He was my first choice for lead climber on our mission, although I would probably need final approval from Emme before assigning anyone the title of "lead" anything on a hike she took part in.

I already knew Rick and Laura brought to the table positive personalities—entirely committed to our hikes and never once complaining about my slower foot speed, which is high praise for mountain-climbing teammates. In fact, they were always upbeat, and they never made the foot speed an issue on our climbs, which is critical to all hikers in a group enjoying the total experience. Even when my driving bounced us around off-road, took us uphill over boulders, or sent us plowing across streams to reach low-access trailheads, there was never a word from either of them. They understood how much fun I had subjecting us to the sharp dips and large rocks of the narrow dirt roads, and never once did I hear anything close to "Slow down!" or "Are you crazy?"

As soon as Pamela caught wind of our intentions to go for four summits with Emme, she conceived that this would be just the kind of story that could work as a local fund-raiser for the Aspen Animal Shelter and the Canine Health Foundation. The Canine Health Foundation is an American Kennel Club institution that funds research to reduce the incidence of inherited diseases in dogs.

When Pamela's idea to include a charity component caught the attention of the *Aspen Times,* the paper ran an article (with photos) announcing that "Emme and her posse" would be attempting to summit four of the state's fourteeners in one day as a fund-raiser:

Hiking for a Doggone Good Cause

Emme Levy Crandall, an Australian terrier and resident of the Roaring Fork Valley, is going to attempt climbing four fourteeners on Saturday, September 6.

Emme and her posse, including her human Dad, Rick Crandall, will depart from Aspen Friday, overnight in Breckenridge, and start off for the hike at 5:30 AM. Emme and Rick have been training all summer for this climb. They would like to make their hike more meaningful by encouraging people to make a pledge for each fourteener to AKC Canine Health Foundation to study and to better understand the health of our dogs, or the Aspen Animal Shelter. A prayer for good weather would also be greatly appreciated. (*Aspen Times,* August 30, 2008)

Based on our team members' schedules, hiking the four peaks would take place on a Saturday, with a caveat of *weather pending,* given that we were only a week removed from the monsoon season that can extend into early September. As was always my preference, we would try to get the earliest possible start in order to be well into our descent when the thunderstorms threatened in the early afternoon. This would mean overnighting in Fairplay, about 160 miles from Aspen, which would leave us about ten miles from the Kite Lake trailhead and the parking area for Mount Democrat—the first of the four fourteeners the next day.

First, a few words about Fairplay—founded in 1859, elevation

9,953 feet, population about 700. Part of the town's charm is the historic district located on a bluff above the South Platte River along Front Street. This is the site of forty-three relocated historical structures brought in from around the state that celebrate the Colorado Gold Rush in an open-air museum called South Park City. For the record, South Park is a basin between two mountain ranges, as well as the name of a fictional town in the TV series *South Park,* created by Trey Parker and Matt Stone, two former University of Colorado Boulder classmates. If your list of must-see Colorado landmarks includes South Park, Fairplay is as close as you're going to get.

We arose early on Saturday and arrived at the trailhead by 6:30 AM—later than our planned start time but still early in the day. The weather forecast was for sun all day and a minimal chance of rain in the higher altitudes. But the combination of the early morning start time and starting off in the shade of the aspens and pines a few hundred feet below the tree line at Kite Lake forced us to deal with temperatures in the mid-twenties, which meant wearing all five layers of clothing I had brought along on the hike. Lightweight layers plus a waterproof windbreaker with a hood is the way to go since layers can be added and swapped out as weather conditions change on the mountain—which is often. As we ascended, the aspens disappeared, and we were surrounded only by evergreens, which shrink to miniature size as we reach the tree line. This was the point in the hike where the views open to the magnificence of this mountain. I have found that mountain peaks can appear both much closer than they are when miles away—as Capitol Peak once did while on a walk with my sister Bev—or well in the distance when it is actually close by, as was in the case of Mount Democrat at this moment.

In the early part of the Mount Democrat ascent, my three hiking partners congregated around me on the trail, since I had done the research and had photos of landmarks that indicated important turns or confirmation that we were headed in the right direction on the most efficient route to the top.

Extreme weather affects all flora, including trees, in higher altitudes. All plant life shrinks in size as you head up. The flowers become miniatures and the trees become dwarfs. You feel like you have become a giant. I had a friend years ago who would hike to timberline to collect trees and make bonsai from them. Without the protection of the trees, the wind immediately made its presence felt, probably lowering the wind chill to about 15 degrees. At the same time, however, we could see the sun line descending down the mountain, trying to meet us halfway as we ascended. As we crossed that line into the full sun at about 13,000 feet, it was as though a kind and considerate someone had turned on the mountain's heating system. It became necessary at that juncture to stop, peel off layers, and aggressively apply sunscreen. With the reflection off the rocks and less atmosphere to block the UVA and UVB rays, sunburns can be severe. Sunscreen is a constant presence on hikes year-round, with my preferred SPF being 30. But as they say, your mileage may vary.

The final 1,000 feet of vertical climb of Mount Democrat was all loose rocks underfoot, which was manageable but tiring. The last thing I wanted to do on this hike was to make news with a face-plant on the rocks or twisting an ankle, so I paid special attention to foot placement. For her part, Emme didn't need hiking sticks or any other equipment from Ute Mountaineer. As was Laura's, Emme's sense of balance was impeccable, and her foot placement was invariably on the stable part of any rock where she was land-ing. Sure, it's a decided advantage to have four legs instead of two, but Emme's natural talents and instincts on mountain trails tran-scended being small and having four legs. Like Gabby Douglas in the middle of a floor routine or Tom Brady on a football field, Emme had both found an activity she passionately loved doing, *and* she excelled at it.

As we got closer to the Democrat summit, the route became rockier still. We stopped briefly to munch on protein bars. Climb-ing requires intense physical exertion, and it's another rookie mis-take on hikes to allow one's energy to wane by failing to replenish protein and carbs. Even more important than protein is water. Dehydration when up that high and exerting that much can take over with consequences that can't be reversed in a short time. With a burst of energy, we made it to the summit. Once again I was overwhelmed with a feeling of exuberance, and Emme looked tri-umphant. Little did she know, it was just the start of things.

Emme at the summit of Mount Democrat,
peak no. 1, in high winds.

We took time to stop and feed ourselves, which for Emme and me meant turkey-and-Swiss sandwiches. I fed Emme at the same intervals I fed (and hydrated) myself, and I cannot recall her once turning down food on a climb.

My partners were in a celebratory mood, but on this day, reaching the summit meant only that we had attained the first of four. We did cluster together in the high wind for a photo with Emme, both for posterity and to prove we'd made it. Each of us extended an index finger to indicate that this was the first summit. Three thousand dollars for charity—and three summits still to go.

The next step was descending the 700 feet down to the Democrat/Cameron saddle and then going for Mount Cameron. Scouting reports told us that except for strong winds—no small "except"—this would be the "easiest" of the four peaks. Had there been a way to save it for last, when the oldest member of the team might be struggling with fatigue, that would have been ideal. But the only way to hike the four peaks by summiting four times was in a set order (Democrat, Cameron, Lincoln, and Bross). It also set up the hike as a loop and, not insignificantly, ended with us descending to our car and not to the other side of the state.

As we had read in reference books and gleaned online, the only challenges in getting to the summit of Cameron at 14,238 feet proved to be about twenty minutes of hiking large rocks and an easy climb to the summit—and the high winds. I'd estimate that the wind was in our faces at a steady 35 mph, with gusts going as high as 45 mph. Not quite the wind strength that could knock over one of us, but when the gusts came at us, it came pretty close. In almost three miles of elevation and at one of the highest points in the Rockies, we had no protection from the elements. There was no place to hide. When the wind blew most forcefully, the only option was to put your head down and push into it.

The extra exertion had me beginning to suck wind and lag behind my hiking colleagues, as I experienced the early warning signs from the Mount Yale hike—when it felt like breathing in a partial vacuum. Fortunately, when I stopped to catch my breath this time, things stabilized in a short time, usually under a minute. The fierce winds at the summit of Mount Cameron ensured that we didn't linger long there. After posing on the second peak, our group descended down to the Lincoln/Cameron side of the saddle, bundled into a circle with Emme in the middle, and feasted on whatever nutrition each of us had brought in our packs. For Emme it would be another turkey-and-cheese sandwich, along with a good amount of water. We were half-way home and set our sights on Mount Lincoln. Unlike New York's (and New Jersey's) Lincoln Tunnel and Manhattan's arts mecca, Lincoln Center, the fourteener is indeed named after the sixteenth and tallest president of the United States, Abraham Lincoln.

After a few hundred feet up Mount Lincoln's rocky summit cone, I began to feel more serious fatigue and a clear lack of energy. By the numbers, Lincoln's was the highest-elevation summit of the four peaks, but starting from the Lincoln/Cameron saddle spared us the climb of the full hike. I speculated that the issue for me was that even after descending to the saddle twice, I had spent the past five hours above 13,000 feet, reducing oxygen to my bloodstream and affecting my lungs and muscles. About halfway up Lincoln, I slowed my progress to ten steps at a time, before I would need to stop, try to breathe, and then resume with another ten steps.

It was my first fourteener with Rick, and he was a generous climbing partner. He alternated between walking out ahead with

Laura and Diana, then hanging back and hiking with me. He would transition between the larger group and me by creating cairns while he waited—stone markers along the trail where other hikers might become confused with their directions.

Having been a search-and-rescue pro, Rick's nature was to be helpful to and protective of others—and cairns became his signature activity on future hikes. The reason I bring along research and photos is that one size didn't always fit all. One person's directional cairns might not always work as well for a climber of lesser skill, so I would carry backup in the form of photos of natural landmarks along the trail to provide us with options.

Rick Peckham making a cairn while waiting for me.

Speaking of options, there were a couple available to me as I made frequent breathing stops. Among items not yet in my pack on Mount Yale was an inhaler normally used for asthma, which I now brought along for breathing emergencies at the suggestion of my family doctor. The other was downing a can of 5-hour Energy, which gave me the caffeine jolt of a sixteen-ounce cup of Starbucks (the "Grande," I believe). After using both, I quickly passed by my climbing buddies who had stopped so I could catch up, and within another minute or so I was 100 feet past them.

The top of the route to Mount Lincoln showed me for the first time what a "false summit" feels like to a hiker. What your eyes see on the trail fools you into believing that the summit is just up ahead and above. But after pushing to get through the rocks and boulders, your reward is…an even higher summit, farther ahead and higher. At the end of a difficult climb, the body relaxes at the false summit, thinking it's done with the uphill climbing, and shifts into downhill mode. It is then that you need to give yourself a pep talk and convince your legs to shift back into climbing mode again.

We reached Mount Lincoln's summit, but not until after some tricky slipping and sliding on the rocky approach. Sections of rocks on the approach are in permanent shade where the icy film on top of them—called verglas—cannot be melted by the sun. This is far less of a problem for Emme, whose extended claws acted like a climber's crampons, the sharp spikes that provide traction on ice. Even though I had recently switched to high-ankle Lowa boots with newly introduced sticky Vibram soles, I was left to jam my feet into the cracks between rocks, creating pressure on each side of the boot. Stepping directly on top of a rock covered by a layer of verglas would send a hiker not wearing crampons dangerously slipping off.

We didn't stay on Lincoln's summit very long. Although the views to the east were stunning even by Colorado standards, it was windy, and all of us were feeling the bite of the cold. This was after having already maxed out on what I had brought to deal with the expected elements—five layers of clothing including my rain jacket

Emme, Laura, and me on the summit of Mount Lincoln, peak no. 3.

as a windbreaker, two pairs of gloves, and a ski hat. Of course, it took just one permanent fur coat—and an orange vest—for the Australian terrier among us to brush aside any weather concerns. Emme's magic number was usually five degrees or colder before waving off a hike. When the ground was so cold as to cause pain to her paws, she'd head back into the house. This did not occur often.

By the time we had descended from Lincoln to the central saddle area, I was battling leg fatigue and was more than slightly dizzy. I knew I probably had enough in the tank for the complete descent to the car, but a Mount Bross ascent looked beyond my strength, though it was only presented 600 feet of elevation. *And it would be the final peak.*

My initial oxygen-deprived suggestion was for the group to take Emme up to the summit of Mount Bross, while I rested and awaited the team's return so we could descend together. After all, the donations were based on the peaks Emme reached—no one cared whether all the humans summited. But this was flawed thinking—there were two ways down to our car from the saddle where I sat: (1) summit Mr. Bross and descend on a new trail or (2) re-summit Mount Democrat —technically the fifth summit that day—and descend using the same trail we took to the saddle that morning. Again, I wasn't thinking clearly. All I knew was that I was completely wiped out.

When there seemed to be no good way of resolving the predicament, and at a time when my thinking was anything but lucid, Emme swung into action again. Only this time her "action" was standing her ground and not moving. When the rest of the team began hiking toward Mount Bross, the fourth peak, Emme would not join the hike unless I was part of the group. She had no way of knowing the donations were based on her climbing; all she knew was that she wasn't going anywhere without me. After losing me once, she had become deeply protective of me on all our climbs together. No matter how much Rick, Diana, and Laura cajoled her and offered her treats, she stuck to her guns. Emme wouldn't budge.

As my thinking became less fuzzy, I decided there was only one way out of this, especially if the goal was to make it back to the parking lot and, eventually, home. I scraped myself off the rock on which I was resting and started the grind to the summit of Mount Bross. Emme immediately got out in front of me to test the trail and lead the way, as we slotted in behind the others. I was moving slowly, but now the weather had improved—a full sun, a calm wind, and that postcard-perfect Colorado-blue sky. In the back of my mind, I knew I needed to cover only 600 feet of elevation, but I never allowed myself to think past a straightforward approach of "one foot after the other"—lift, step, push up, and then repeat again with the other foot. I kept it simple, figuring it was no use counting steps or even looking up to check the distance to the summit. It was one rocky step at a time, and let's see where that takes us.

In the end, we summited Mount Bross at 14,172 feet, and I must admit this summit felt sweet. Inspired by my vigilant, loyal, and stubborn dog, I had climbed well beyond my physical limits and wound up reaching new heights. My hiking pals insisted that I pose solo with Emme on the summit rocks, holding up four fingers to signify that we had scaled all four peaks. It was all about completing our mission successfully, and I was enormously proud of what our group accomplished as a team and as individuals.

With the four peaks in the record book and the fund-raising component documented with photos, we all got together for the trip down the mountain and to the parking lot. The excitement and the short rest had given me strength for the descent. Realizing there was no more uphill made me so happy that my disposition on the trail might have even crossed into the category of cheery and downright jabber-mouthed. I don't talk on the way up a climb, but when descending from a summit—you won't get a word in edgewise.

After a long day of dealing with my own stamina issues, my attention as we descended focused on Emme. Heading down directly from Bross toward the trailhead presented us with a new trail, and it turned out to be an ugly, steep, and loose scree-laden slope. I was concerned about Emme's paw pads getting cut up on the sharp edges, so I stopped often to check them. Remarkably,

Mount Bross, the fourth fourteener summit of the day.

her paws had no damage or cuts at all after eight hours of mountain trails of sharp rocks, a credit to her precise foot placement.
Her game plan was to move from rock to rock, sometimes angling
sideways and other times temporarily reversing when she didn't
like what she saw. Following her in general was a sound plan for
many reasons, especially on this day as she intuitively found flat-
ter rock surfaces for a more stable foot fall.

By 3:30 PM, and after almost nine hours of hiking, we had made
it back to the car. We had done it. Four peaks in one day had been
one of our best and most satisfying adventures yet. As the team
relived the day's experiences over pizza and beer when we got
closer to home, we raised a toast to Emme, who had further established herself as a highly skilled and durable climber of fourteeners.
She also added the credential of effective fund-raiser, having raised
$16,000 in donations (plus $2,000 contributed after the climb) for
the Aspen Animal Shelter and the Canine Health Foundation.

Adding the four fourteeners served as a nice confidence boost to end the 2008 hiking season. I would need that motivation—as well as an occasional peek at the *Aspen Times*—to remind myself why my body required daily workouts on the moguls, in snowshoes, and in the gym. I wanted more fourteeners—dozens of them and, if possible, more difficult ones.

Another motivation was my seven-year-old hiking partner, Emme. Just when I'd believe she was at the top of her mountain-climbing game, she would break out brand-new moves and improved techniques based on what she continued to learn on each hike. Her joyful spirit and uncanny dexterity on the trails made this a special time of our lives for both of us to enjoy. It was a time to live in the present and in the world of the possible. I needed to stay in shape so we both could continue doing what we loved so much—hiking on all kinds of trails and sometimes reaching the top of 14,000-foot mountains.

CHAPTER 10

A TALE OF TWO BULLS

*Of all the paths you take in life, make sure
a few of them are dirt.*

—John Muir

*Three buds—brother Wayne, son Brett, and me.
The day for the Snowmass climb started with great optimism.*

On a winter high after Emme and I had reached the summits of four separate fourteeners on one magical September day, I allowed myself to occasionally daydream of what we could do for an encore. I have always been a big believer in taking on new challenges and ratcheting up the stakes, which set the range of possibilities for our next hike somewhere between attempting five peaks in a single day and climbing Mount Everest.

It had been difficult to ignore the clamoring of the media, asking what would be next for us. Okay, I had run into a reporter for the *Aspen Times* who might have mentioned seeing the newspaper accounts of Emme and our team hiking four peaks for charity. But I have always thrived when focused on the next achievement, not dwelling on what happened in the past. I know grown men who still bring up a big pass they caught in a high school JV football game, as though nothing had occurred to match that feat in the intervening fifty years. We need to remember that Bruce Springsteen's song "Glory Days" is a cautionary tale; Springsteen himself has stayed at the top by constantly planning the next move, most recently how to (brilliantly) tell his life story from a Broadway stage.

For all my off-season research and trip planning leading to what would be next, the two hikes that defined the summer of 2009 took place in July and came together on short notice. They involved two of my three younger siblings—my sister Beverly and my brother Wayne. The remaining details of the two excursions—the settings, hiking distance, difficulty of the trail, the cast of characters, and the stories themselves—could not have been more dissimilar. What links them, however, is that they are two among a handful of hikes I will remember and talk about for the rest of my life.

The first of the two hikes came as the result of an all-too-brief vacation visit from Beverly, who has spent her entire life married to the same wonderful man and living in Dallas. She, too, has found later-life passions, which include her roles as an enthusiastic grandparent and that of a highly skilled bridge player, a game at which she has advanced to Bronze Life Master and now teaches on a part-time basis. Bev is also the glue that keeps the four siblings close since the passing of our parents, organizing gatherings on a major holiday that allowed the four of us and our spouses—including our brother Jerry from West Chester, Pennsylvania—to come together annually as a group.

Bev celebrating a great day hiking, with the most challenging fourteener in the Rockies, Capitol Peak, still seven miles in the distance to her left.

Hiking in the mountains is what people ask to do when they visit Aspen in the summer, and Beverly, who had met Emme several years ago, had yet to witness our Aussie terrier in action on a trail. The route I chose was one of my favorites for family and friends visiting town—and one I knew she would love—a beautiful five-mile round trip with a gradual incline, all in the shadow of the ever-present, hovering profile of Capitol Peak. Remember my theory about mountain peaks seeming either far closer or much farther away than they really are? Capitol Peak felt as though we could touch it, despite our starting the short hike seven miles from the trailhead, another seven miles from its namesake lake and yet another three dicey and dangerous miles from the lake to the summit. Things may be bigger in Texas, but they don't have anything close to Capitol Peak.

We happened to be hiking on a weekday, and not far into the trail, Bev started to look around. "Where are all the hikers?" she asked, pointing out that we had seen just two other people after walking nearly a mile. When there were breaks in our conversation, she called my attention to the audible buzzing of the bees, then wondered about all the sounds of nature that were drowned out by the daily din of city noise.

The quiet setting lent itself to a deeper and more personal conversation than Beverly and I had experienced in a long time. For the first time, we talked at length about her serious commitment to the game of bridge, a game she took up while in her forties. It was cool to hear her describe her upbeat approach to every hand— "There is a way to make this work." She said these eight words have formed a mind-set that she has been able to successfully apply to many of her life's problems away from the bridge table.

Bev and I then compared our later-life passions—her mastery of bridge and my intense devotion to mountain climbing. "Just when you think you've made it," she said, "the game will humble you and fill you with self-doubt." She could just as easily have been describing my struggle with the demands of a 14,000-foot, Class 3 mountain trail.

As Bev and I kept walking and talking, we noticed occasional cow pies—and not the kind they make on the Food Network. These pies were the poop (using the scientific vernacular) generated by the cows and bulls a local rancher had permission to graze in the surrounding meadows. Indeed, we soon came upon a group of them, all black, extremely healthy-looking, and not particularly concerned with our merry band of hikers. The fields of wildflowers and the glorious, sunny day provided the perfect setting for us to continue to catch up on one another's lives. Bev is five years younger than me, and I am thrilled we have remained close, going back sixty years to when I assigned myself the task of teaching her the names of the U.S. presidents in numerical order.

It was a little farther up the trail, however, that we came upon a scene that brought all conversation and forward progress to an abrupt halt—two full-size bulls facing down one another in what seemed to be the middle of the field. What we didn't immediately realize was that they were on opposite sides of the continuation of our winding hiking path. That these bulls were polled—meaning they didn't have horns—made them only slightly less dangerous to humans. With running speeds that can rival a horse's, one of those bulls could have caused severe injury and even death by deciding to abandon the bull-versus-bull battle to chase and stomp on us instead. Each probably weighed over 2,000 pounds, the best estimate I could offer short of interrupting the festivities to perform body measurements and run the formulas.

Although not an animal behaviorist, I feared it might not be long before our animal friends ceased the preliminaries and advanced to violent head-butting. While our solution might come about as the result of a double knockout, we had no desire to witness this battle—a pushing contest similar to four-legged sumo wrestling, only without the *mawashi* (the loincloth) ringside. Whatever was about to transpire, nothing about the current behavior could be interpreted as remotely friendly, nor did it look as though they would be taking a short break from their bellicosity anytime soon to allow the three of us to pass.

A rule of thumb—let's call it the Pamplona's Law—is that unless it is a condition of employment, never allow yourself within fifty feet of a bull unless there is a wall or at least a strong fence involved. This

The head-butting bulls, up close. Emme is on the path in the foreground.

goes double for a bull that might be agitated, a category for which both path-blocking, head-butters plainly qualified. My response to the bovine standoff was to look for detours, but the available alternate routes would have entailed bushwhacking through weeds that would have been unkind to our bare legs. Chatty up until this point, Beverly stood speechless, amazed at how suddenly our hike and the bulls' skirmish had converged to form a perfect stalemate. It was quickly looking as though we would have no choice but to turn around and find another hiking path in the area.

This was the exact moment when Emme decided she had seen enough. Leading the hike as usual, she proceeded to walk to within about fifteen feet of the action and let out one of her deep-throated *rrruffs.* As Bev still describes it, Emme's message—a combination of naïveté or cleverness—was *Ready or not, I'm coming through, and I'm blazing a trail for my humans.*

The bulls immediately broke form and both heads turned to check out the source of the odd sound. With the self-assurance of one who owned the space, Emme then gave them the stare that by this time had built a nine-year track record of successful intimidation across the animal kingdom. I started chuckling to myself at the thought of a twenty-pound alpha dog believing she could do something about 4,000 pounds of ill-humored cattle blocking our path. But Emme, who often barked skyward to chastise Mother Nature for sending thunderstorms, wasn't about to be deterred by a couple of oversized brutes engaging in a territorial scrap.

Had I not returned with photo evidence, I would not expect anyone to believe the play-by-play of what happened next. The bulls immediately backed up from the trail until they were each about a half-dozen feet off the path to either side. It was like watching two eighteen-wheeler trucks backing out of an intersection. The bulls appeared calm, as Emme continued to stare them down. Cutting me a *Let's get while the gettin's good* side glance, Emme never slowed down and walked past the animals as though this were her territory and not the other way around. Without hesitation, I followed Emme, with Bev behind me muttering, "But, but . . ." Her understandable concern was that the bulls' *ad hoc* truce might end precisely at the exact instant we happened to be walking between them. Good point, I thought, so we picked up the pace, passing within ten feet of where each of them flanked us. Neither bull so much as flinched, although their large eyes did regard us with what appeared to be mild curiosity. About fifteen seconds after making it through the gauntlet we heard rustling sounds behind us—the bulls had returned to their head-to-head standoff. The ceasefire Emme had negotiated was already history. Amazingly, we had made it to the other side.

After we had safely cleared the bulls and let out a collective exhale, I recall Bev asking, "Who the heck do you think you are, little Emme?" and getting no answer, although I found it all to be hilarious. It led to a discussion about the possible origins of Emme's pure chutzpah—her lupine heritage and instincts? Or a lifetime of being delusional about her size? Or all of the above?

To this day, Bev will insist that unless she had witnessed in person Emme's parting of the bulls, "There is no way you would have gotten me to believe that story." We always laugh, and I admit to her that even as someone who had been on hand for all Emme's Greatest Hits, Volumes 1 and 2, clearing the hiking path by growling and staring down the bulls might have been her finest hour and coolest trick yet.

While I cannot recommend Emme's game plan for dealing with the bulls, there was much to learn from my hundreds of hikes with her. Whether it was a one-miler along the river, an impromptu winter charge up the trail behind our home, or four 14,000-foot peaks in one day, she was ecstatic to be outdoors and hiking, always finding genuine joy in each new experience. Following her lead over many years had resulted in mountain climbing becoming my life's passion. But the second part of her lesson was equally as important—to be grateful for and revel in every adventure, both large and small. For Emme, the mountains weren't defined by numbers, and there were no inconsequential missions. It didn't matter whether it was a trail we'd followed hundreds of times, our old Zen hideout up on Independence Pass, or a challenging fourteener she was seeing for the first time—when Emme was on a hike, she was the happiest creature on God's Earth. She never stopped teaching me to stop, smell the wildflowers, and appreciate each moment of every day.

These were lessons I would need on a hike just two weeks after our encounter with the bulls. During the same week, my son Brett had made plans to come to town for our annual fourteener together, my brother Wayne had issued a challenge: choose a difficult fourteener, and he would fly in from his home in Scottsdale. What he lacked in formal mountain climbing skills Wayne overcame by being strong and extremely athletic. He also had (relative) youth on his side, clocking in at fifteen years younger than me. Brett's five years of experience and expertise of technical climbing on the most difficult of the fourteeners gave me the confidence to go along with Wayne's wish and choose a mountain that was at the edge of my comfort zone.

The search for a difficult climb our group could summit kept coming back to 14,092-foot Snowmass Mountain, not to be confused with one of the four mountains that form the Aspen/Snowmass ski resort. Rated Class 3 for its steep, loose rocks and extensive boulder fields, Snowmass looked like a more challenging fourteener I could manage, especially with Brett as part of our team. When I invited our hiking pal Laura to be our fourth, she accepted in a heartbeat, reporting that she would have made it to the mountain's summit the prior year had her group not run out of daylight.

There was another challenge on this climb for which I was also a rookie and made mistakes. The approach to the base of the mountain was the longest of any fourteener, eight and a half miles and 3,000 feet up just to get up to Snowmass Lake. For the first time, we were going to backpack up and camp at the lake for an early morning start on the climb the next day. That meant a bigger backpack loaded with tent, sleeping bag, food, and other extras. My pack was heavy and the hike was long, but when I first loaded up, I felt I could handle it.

Based on descriptions of the mountain conditions and the blog posts, which issued strong advisories against attempting to climb Snowmass with a dog, we made Emme a healthy scratch for this outing. This created the trip's first serious challenge before I'd even made it out of the driveway—sneaking out of the house with my full hiking gear and convincing Emme I was on a business trip. In addition to keeping tabs on the status of her own hiking uniform, she kept an even closer watch on my gear, for any number of reasons. As I drove to Snowmass, I wondered what Emme was thinking at that moment: *We take gear on hikes. Wait, there's no gear in the house. What does this mean? It can't be good.* But as whip-smart as I believed Emme to be, I never allowed myself to believe she'd figured out that we had failed to include her on a mountain hike.

The hike did not turn out as planned. Brett warned me that I had overloaded my backpack, and I felt my hips and back give out at about the five-mile mark—with another three and a half miles and a thousand feet of elevation to go in order to reach Snowmass Lake. Soon, I could no longer advance even short distances on the ascent. Since the others had gone well ahead, I carved out a message in the path should any of them come looking for me, then began the return trip to the parking lot.

About two miles into the descent I heard Brett running down the path from above. He had taken his backpack off and sprinted three miles down the mountain to check on me. When I expressed astonishment that he had come so far to find me, his reply was pure Brett. "Hey," he said. "I've got only one dad. What did you think I would do?" He offered to carry my pack back up to the lake and campground, but at that point I was too tired for another ascent attempt, even minus the backpack. Also, I was bitterly disappointed that my body had given out and let me down. After a brief discussion, Brett agreed that I should continue to the car, while he would head back up to lead Wayne and Laura on a summit attempt the next day.

As I hiked down the final two miles, I dealt with a barrage of doubts and questions I have asked myself before. About to turn sixty-six in a few weeks, was I becoming too old for high-altitude climbing? Rarely would I see men or women my age hiking challenging fourteeners, and perhaps there were sound reasons for this. Was I not accepting the realities of the calendar? I put aside age for the moment and began focusing on factors I could control. For example, I did have the power to better manage my weight. My stats of 6'1" and 200 pounds had served me well for many years. But those years were not spent hiking high-elevation mountain trails, where every pound was a net drag.

I had never accepted limits in my life. Would I have to start now? The conundrum is that while I am as old as I've ever been, this moment is also as young as I will ever be from now until check-out time. There is no time to waste. As Robin Williams says in *Dead Poets Society,* "Carpe diem. Seize the day, boys."

I strongly believe that it is consistent with the American entre-preneurial spirit not to be slowed or embarrassed by failing but to treat it as a necessary step to success. Or, as Henry Ford said, "the opportunity to begin again, only this time more wisely." By the time I reached the car, I had decided that I would begin a plan to lose weight starting with my next meal. I would also call the next day to make an appointment to see a pulmonologist about the reduced lung capacity issues that had been diagnosed back in Michigan. The condition hadn't affected life in Ann Arbor, my activities on vacations, or even living in our current home at 8,500 feet of elevation. But oxygen absorption numbers diminish quickly at high altitudes, and perhaps high-stress exercise at 14,000 feet was the breaking point at which my reduced lung capacity became exposed.

Back at home I went on a no-white nutritional program (no salt, sugar, potatoes, bread, pasta, rice, White Russians) except for flaky fish. I also cut out packaged products, which typically contain all kinds of hidden ingredients designed to make you become addicted to them. For instance, there are sixty-one names for sugar on food packaging—agave nectar, corn syrup, fructose, glucose, maltodextrin, muscovado, saccharose, sorghum, treacle ... the list goes on. It's all sugar, all bad. Gradually, it was no longer a matter of withholding foods I once ate; I convinced myself I no longer liked or wanted them. Friends now looked to me to help them study labels of products to see both how much sugar they contained and where, if not listed, sugar was hiding in any of its several disguises. I'm talking to you, fructose.

Within three months, I had exceeded my goal and lost twenty-five pounds. On my next fourteener, I would be packing a special inhaler from the pulmonologist, and high-tech lightweight gear that took my pack weight down thirteen pounds. I couldn't wait to see how it would feel to be carrying so much less of me on a fourteener. That I eagerly awaited the challenge of the next fourteener was an understatement. Based on correctable physical and medical issues I needed to address in order to continue high-altitude hiking, the Snowmass episode had already been officially moved to the "win" column.

Having lived long enough to recall when sixty-six-year-old men were elderly looking and dying of natural causes, I considered myself blessed to still be able to hike the highest mountain peaks in the country. As I saw it, a high number next to my name should be no reason to cut back on our adventures. If the payoff for diligently maintaining fitness and nutrition levels would be more time in the mountains with Emme, then bring it on. I would be prepared to make the sacrifices and pay whatever price it took to extend our days and experiences on the hiking trails.

As she gained experience navigating fields of boulders more

than double her size, Emme learned that the best way forward is sometimes found by taking two steps back. It is a lesson she has passed along to me. The plan responsible for my health reboot was hatched on the way back down the trail from a hike I was forced to abandon. Retreat to move ahead, keep failing forward in order to succeed. Or maybe, as Samuel Beckett said, it is enough to "fail better." It certainly had been an eventful offseason, and I couldn't wait to be sitting again at 14,000 feet with Emme and pondering the new lessons we learned on every trip to the mountains.

CHAPTER 11

EMME THE RESCUE DOG

I seldom end up where I wanted to go, but almost always end up where I need to be.

—Douglas Adams, *The Long, Dark Tea Time of the Soul*

Emme is waiting for me on the way to Mount Princeton. The summit is above the snow gullies in the far distance.

After my third offseason conditioning program that culminated with climbing Tiehack with Emme every other day for almost two months, I now understand why baseball players and managers can become so exasperated during the final stages of spring training. They want the real games to begin—and so do I. With all due respect to the hundreds of hiking paths, nature walks, skiing trails, and scenic roads available in the Rocky Mountains, the focus at this stage of my life was on hiking fourteeners.

There were more question marks than usual, heading into the 2010 summer hiking season. The next mountain we choose will be Emme's first fourteener since she ascended to four 14,000-foot summits in one day for charity back on September 6, 2008. For me, it will be the first fourteener since I hit the wall and needed to turn around only half way up the Snowmass Mountain hike the previous July.

Despite my missing out on what seemed like a terrific two days of camping, overnighting, and hiking, the Snowmass mess brought about many positives. The five-mile walk-of-shame down the mountain was just long enough for me to identify problems and commit to solving them as soon as I rejoined civilization. Each year I got older, the fourteeners seemed to get higher. I could not control the march of time. But I addressed the issues I could control that would keep me on the mountains with my dog, and I was anxious to test-drive my new-and-improved self on a fourteener. I didn't allow myself to consider next steps if I were to hit the wall and needed to turn back on the next hike. I was running out of variables within my control that could be improved through hard work and resolve.

Then one day I decided that the hike that made perfect sense for Emme and me based on where things stood right now was Mount Princeton. In terms of difficulty of climbing, it was a notch or two or three above both Mount Yale, our first fourteener, and the Democrat/Cameron/Lincoln/Bross superfecta we had scaled over a year and a half ago.

In a decade of trips over the Trout Creek Pass, we had been treated to the stunning, towering gray summit of Mount Princeton that appears to rise abruptly from the front of the 4Runner and then from the valley floor as one continues up the road's steady incline. Unattached to other peaks and ridges and framed between two U-shaped glacier valleys for maximum effect, Mount Princeton is by far the most dominant mountain of the Sawatch Range. You simply cannot ignore it as you drive on Highway 24 through Buena Vista on the other side of Independence Pass or when heading west on U.S. Highway 285 and into the Arkansas River Valley.

Ranked nineteenth in elevation among Colorado's fourteeners, Mount Princeton is the southernmost of the nine so-called Collegiate Peaks that each measure over 14,000 feet and, on a typical Colorado sunny day, it is visible from distances of well over one hundred miles. Like most of the Collegiate Peaks, Mount Princeton was renamed by renowned mapmaker Henry Gannett, who was also one of the founders of the National Geographic Society and part of Josiah Whitney's 1869 expedition. Fun fact: the first person to officially summit Mount Princeton was a Princeton graduate, William Libbey, in 1877. It's also worth mentioning that at age fifty-seven, Libbey won a silver medal at the 1912 Olympics in Stockholm as a member of the U.S. Rifle Team. We are proud that Mr. Libbey was another member of the club that considered age to be just a number.

Although there are pull-offs and access roads for cars, many drivers simply cannot help themselves at the sight of Mount Princeton and can often be seen parked on the shoulders of Highways 24 and 285, taking photographs. Mount Princeton was a feast for the eyes—the rose-colored pinks and reds of early morning's first light, the steep ridges backlit by brilliant sunsets, and the radiant shimmer of the snow-covered peaks.

"Someday," I often promised myself, "I will climb that mountain." By late May, I had been unable to put off "someday" any longer. With Father's Day in mind and early July filling up with events revolving around the Fourth of July in Aspen, I booked the date, June 24, and recruited my hiking buddies, Laura and Shan, to make the hike with Emme and me.

During the week leading up to the big day, however, both Laura and Shan dropped out due to various commitments. But being more fired up than I have ever been to start a hiking season, I never gave serious thought to canceling or even postponing. With the benefit of hindsight, the decision to climb a fourteener without another human along might have been a questionable call and one I made with too much heart and not enough brain. The only explanation I can give is that after almost a year of training for the fourteener that would erase the memory of Snowmass, I was not about to call off the hike. And after wearing out Tiehack and any number of local twelves and thirteeners with Emme in the months leading up to Mount Princeton, another hike with her on a mountain did not register with me as a solo flight. It would also be my first hike with a GPS device that sent my location to a monitored personal website every ten minutes. These have become essential on our mountain climbs, particularly as the technology has improved since the GPS's earliest iterations.

I looked at Emme and said, "You are going to give me a Father's Day present. We're going for Mount Princeton solo—just you and me." Hiking Mount Princeton with Emme would be an early Father's Day gift to myself and the best possible way to spend a day for Emme. This demanding climb would also be an objective yardstick for where I stood after being unable to handle Snowmass Mountain and after spending the past year questioning if someone my age could still handle fourteeners.

The Mount Princeton hike began with one of Emme's favorite rituals—bunking at the hotel room in Buena Vista less than five miles from the trailhead on the night before the hike. As I have mentioned, foot speed is not my strong suit on the mountain, so I compensate by starting my hikes as early in the morning as possible, thus reducing the possibility of being caught in an afternoon thunderstorm. Besides failing to get an early start, another frequent amateur mistake related to the thunderstorms is taking an extended victory lap on the summit. If you see clouds forming, take a *short* rest, eat a sandwich—and feed one to your dog—then start the descent, remembering to retrace the direction from which you came up.

Or, as in my case, when in doubt, you follow your dog.

The recommended starting point to this climb is a smallish pull-off on an old silver mining road near two old radio towers. The darkness soon gave way to a brilliant red and pink sunrise, a bonus from Mother Nature for getting an early start. The hike started on the remains of a road toward a silver mine but then turned sharply into the rocks. For the rest of the ascent, it would turn out to be rocks all the way. It is exhausting and will make route-finding a true adventure. There are occasional cairns to show the way, but because they are stacked with the same gray stones as make up the rest of the mountain, they don't stand out as they do on other trails and require extra diligence. Fortunately, my companion for the day has superpowers at sniffing out where people have been before.

All fourteeners require homework and preparation. But shortly into the Mount Princeton hike, it became clear that we would be working with minimally-marked trails, combined with online scouting reports that turned out to be sketchy at best. For instance, one snippet read, "Trail climbs through rocks." What "trail" were they talking about? The small sections of trail that existed regularly went into hiding and often simply disappeared. And there was no climbing "through rocks"—as I said, the entire hike took place *on* rocks. The ranking system for climbs grades a mountain based on its worst pitch, so I was expecting a minimal amount of the climb to be Class 2, with the remainder being Class 1 (easiest rank). It turned out to be a Class 2 hike all the way, with rocks from start to finish. In short, the hike was neither what was described nor what I had planned for.

On a happy note, I had never felt better or more in control on a fourteener hike than I did on that ascent to Mount Princeton. While I didn't feel as though I were twenty-five again, the lung and leg trouble for which I had been on high alert after Snowmass was a no-show on this trail. My overall pace felt even faster than on previous fourteeners—still slow, modest, whatever you want to call it—albeit with clearer lungs and more controlled breathing. Not

Here Emme is rocking on a teetering rock, I think to show me not to climb on it.

that hiking at a leisurely clip didn't have its rewards, as it allowed me to be constantly amazed by the perseverance of every shred of nature that had managed to sustain its life and beauty along the rugged terrains of these stunning trails. It allowed me to get to know the mountain on a different level, as a new and unforgettable friend with a real personality.

To the surprise of no one, Emme showed up on opening day in mid-season form, landing her boulder-to-boulder jumps perfectly and making sense of a trail that was busy feeding up a steady diet of curveballs. Then, from about 13,600 feet to 14,000 feet, the trail turned steeper, and the rocks became even more unstable. When we finally scrambled over the final section to reach the summit, it was 12:15 PM. We had been hiking for five hours and fifteen glorious minutes. The pace had been slow, but my body came through the test with flying colors. We had climbed Mount Princeton, at least the uphill—and more demanding—leg of an impressive fourteener, and we were still feeling terrific.

As she had done when we attained the summit of every thirteener or fourteener, Emme sought out the highest rock, stood on it, and stared out far into the distance. On a clear day from the summit of Mount Princeton, you can see forever—which at this moment was more than half (about thirty) of Colorado's fourteeners. Emme's stance approximated the pose she used when riding on the console of the 4Runner and staring out the windshield at the road ahead. Was she thinking deep thoughts about the universe, or plotting out new-and-improved pursuit tactics to employ against the marmots and ptarmigans? For my part, I ate a peanut butter and jelly sandwich (turkey-and-Swiss for Emme) and thought about the past eleven months of wondering if I would ever be at the summit of a fourteener again. My mind then wandered to a recent altitude re-designation by the Colorado Geological Survey that had increased the elevation of Mount Princeton to 14,204 feet from 14,197 feet. All the books and official records that would need to be changed—*for seven feet?* It's a rounding error at first blush, until you realize it's equivalent to the height of Fezzik in *The Princess Bride,* a role played brilliantly by the late pro wrestler, André the Giant. The mind goes to curious places at 14,204 feet.

These and other mysteries would need to wait. The purpose of the 4:00 AM alarm and 6:00 AM start to the hike was to preempt the drama where the deliberate (a.k.a. slow-moving) hiker and his much faster but loyal dog are racing a dangerous thunderstorm past the tree line and down a mountain trail. To reinforce the seriousness of the threat, there is a plaque about fifty feet from the summit of Mount Princeton that marks the spot where an avid and experienced Colorado outdoorswoman, Catherine Pugin, was struck and killed by lightning in 1995.

Having taken over five hours to negotiate the confusing trails of all rocks on our way to the summit, I anticipated a descent of at least three hours, possibly longer. Making one's way down from a Class 2 mountain doesn't take as long, but the descent does place additional pressure on quads, knees, ankles, and calf muscles. This will be exacerbated by the all-rock—and loose rock—surface in the higher altitudes of Mount Princeton that will require a variety of foot positions, landings, and side-stepping. But not long into our return trip, it became clear that we were in for another action-packed afternoon on a Collegiate Peaks fourteener. Fortunately, on this day I was breathing normally at high altitudes, allowing us to offer aid to a trio of hikers who found themselves in sticky situations.

First, we came upon a young man at 13,200 feet, incoherent and nearly passed out in the baking sun. He was also sunburned and breathing hard, no surprise since we were above the tree line, which left him completely unprotected from the sun's rays. Based on his rambling story, he had been in a group of four inexperienced hikers who had the goal of "summit or bust." When this fellow decided he couldn't continue, his three pals resumed the hike without him, making slapdash meet-up plans for a rendezvous with him. "They said they would meet me here," he said. "But now I forget where 'here' is."

The young man had made his plans three hours earlier, while exhausted in the thin air, and on a mountain with no clear trails. Not only was it an uncommonly warm day at the high altitude, the light gray sea of rocks reflected the rays of the sun up onto anyone who happened to be hiking or, in the case of our unfortunate friend, sitting. Between the rays from above and the heat from below, the young man was slowly being cooked by a combination of a grill and an oven. It was time to get him off the mountain.

My top-of-the-trail diagnosis of him was dehydration and exhaustion at very least, with a slight chance of acute mountain sickness—any one of which is a major concern at this altitude and several miles from the trailhead. Our new friend was also heavyset, which no doubt combined with Colorado's thin air to contribute to his breathing difficulties, particularly if he had not acclimatized. When I offered him water, he declined, proudly showing me a hydration bladder and pointing at a stainless-steel water bottle, both of which were nearly full.

"I have plenty of water," he said.

Those words set off red flags. Yes, he had plenty of water—in his pack—and this meant he hadn't been drinking any. Along with the abridged lecture on dehydration ("Once you're thirsty, it's probably too late."), I demanded that he start drinking water immediately. I also recommended in strong terms that he needed to follow us off the mountain as quickly as possible or risk a serious health crisis. "I'll be okay," he kept saying. "I'm fine here."

In the end, despite my no-nonsense insistence that he follow us, he refused to come down the mountain without his friends. As he and I were conversing, Emme briefly diverted from the path and led us to a rock overhang that offered shade. Did she know the man needed it, or was she seeking shade for herself? Maybe both.

After I helped the man reach that spot Emme had found, our new friend plopped into the shade and, upon getting off his feet, assured us he was feeling better. "Are you sure?" I asked. "I'm cool," said the man, telling a far different story with his face and body language. "Are you sure?" I asked again. "I'm sure," he said. He again waved us off, and we wished him well.

Shortly afterward, at about 13,000 feet, we came upon two young women who looked to be in their early twenties. They were also both unsure on their feet and looking confused. The women also appeared to be suffering from acute sunburn that had left their faces the color of freshly-steamed Maine lobsters. Above the tree line of Mount Princeton, the trail becomes a matter of guesswork, especially early in the season and immediately after snowmelt and fresh rock fall. As with the young man, these women had also lost their bearings on an agreed-upon meeting place with hiking partners who had left them to continue to the summit.

"We were supposed to meet them at a cave we passed on the way up," said one finally, adding that she believed it to be located near where the trees ended. No lecture this time, but I did share my sunscreen, which they lathered all over their faces and necks. Both women were fair-skinned, and I couldn't help but wish they'd had access to the sunscreen an hour or two earlier in the day.

"Do you know the way down from here?" one of them soon asked, pointing at the trail. "Sure. Follow me," I answered, but both hesitated, understandably wary of tagging along with a lone male stranger on a remote mountain trail. Both women also complained of feeling light-headed and groggy, which also might have contributed to their reticence.

Seeking to put them at ease, I said, "Emme knows the way, let's follow her."

Maybe they thought I was making a joke, but it seemed to do the trick. When Emme took my cue and began to march down the trail, they glanced at each other and decided to follow the leader.

As our group of four began hiking downhill, it felt like a summer stock theater company's interpretation of *The Wizard of Oz*, with Emme playing the role of Toto who, for trivia fans, was played in the film by Terry, a female brindle Cairn terrier.

Reminiscent of all five dogs who played Lassie on TV, Emme swung into full rescue-dog mode, as though the job were part of her DNA. She unwaveringly led us down the often-disappearing rocky trail segments, stopping every fifty feet to make sure she didn't get too far ahead of her followers, laboring behind her. It was a curious, slow-moving procession, with the young women following Emme and me following the entire group.

"Is she always like this?" asked the taller of the women, gesturing ahead at Emme, who had again stopped to allow our group to catch up with her before continuing down the path.

"Every. Single. Day," I replied. I told her that had we been sitting around a campfire instead of descending a treacherous, rocky trail of a 14,000-foot mountain, I would have regaled her with stories about bears, porcupines, and head-butting bulls.

Slowing us down when we reached snow gullies, I was glad to see that the sun had warmed the white stuff enough to allow me to kick good steps across the steep ribbons of snow.

This time it was my turn to pause the hike. Knowing that the women were struggling physically with heat exhaustion, I emphasized the importance of maintaining their balance.

"You both need to be mindful of where you land every step," I told them. "Especially since you're both a bit wobbly."

"Got it," they both replied.

Taking the lead now with Emme, I then made level tracks horizontally across the snow gullies so the women could walk exactly in my steps and avoid slipping. I reminded them that the consequence of one slip would be a hard-to-stop slide down the snow and into the rocks, an outcome we unanimously agreed must be avoided.

Resuming our earlier hiking order on the trail after passing the snow, I became concerned about Emme's short legs and her body being so close to the gray, reflecting rocks. The rocks, however, never became so hot as to be untouchable, and I never once noticed Emme in distress from heat or licking her paw pads. As I continued to stop and check both the heat of the rocks and the effects on Emme's stomach and paws, she looked up and gave me an eye roll that seemed to say *Keep hiking. I'll let you know when there's a problem.*

Then, right above the tree line, after a sudden pause for a round of serious sniffing, Emme veered slightly off-trail, leading us to a rocky overhang that might provide shade and cooling. It didn't look like the cave they had been describing to me, but one of the women reacted immediately.

"You found it! You found it!" she shouted to Emme. *Of course I did* was Emme's expression, as her eyes appeared to match the joy of the two suddenly jubilant women.

Improbably, the women agreed that this was the *exact* spot where they had made plans to reunite with their friends. It was also the second cave/overhang Emme had found for people in distress and needing shelter in one afternoon. There was just enough room under the ledge for both women to safely get off their feet while also being shielded from the sun. Finding the cave seemed to energize the women, who reassured me that they would remain at the meeting place for now and figure out next steps later.

"Thank you, Emme," said the grateful women several times and in stereo.

Despite having long since missed the appointed time with their friends, they were adamant about staying where they were. After they insisted for the third or fourth time, they were settled and more than adequately hydrated, I could only reply, "Then I guess our work is done here." Emme and I then continued down the mountain, back to the trailhead and the towers we had last seen at 6 AM, almost nine hours earlier.

As for Mount Princeton, it was a magnificent day, even factoring in the loose rocks, the non-trail trails, and the five-hour trip to the top. Not to mention the drama in stumbling upon the three climbers in distress as we made our descent. But after years of watching Mount Princeton regally rise from the hood of my car on Highway 82, we had gone to the top and did it our way—no real struggle and lots of beauty at the summit. It was in the books.

Mount Princeton was my first fourteener hike with Emme after last summer's Snowmass turn-back, and Emme's first fourteener in almost two years. We both had pulled it off without a hitch. After last summer's temporary setback, the climb had been a useful yardstick for determining where I stood right now and what would continue to be possible. If we were going to continue to be fourteener climbers, we needed to kick things into gear. Neither of us was getting any younger.

As for Emme, instead of taking a well-deserved rest, she decided to punctuate a long day of high-altitude climbing—one that probably required hundreds of thousands of perfectly landed steps—by chasing a marmot for a lap or two around the car. Hunting, after all, is what Aussie terriers do, and she had likely ignored dozens of varmints just off the trail as she led the three overheated hikers down from the top of Mount Princeton. Now, with everyone safe and her rescue-dog duties at a successful end, she couldn't resist the opportunity to chase the animal back into its hole before it tried to steal my hiking sticks. It seemed to complete the day for her. We were both exactly where we wanted to be.

CHAPTER 12

OUR LAST HIKES

The only way of discovering the limits
of the possible is to venture a little way
past them into the impossible.

—Arthur C. Clarke

One happy guy, going for a fourteener summit every time
the weather forecast was good for two days in a row.

In the days following our Mount Princeton hike, I felt as well as I ever have in my life—both physically and mentally. After being unable to continue after five miles on Snowmass Mountain eleven months earlier, I purposely chose a difficult fourteener as the next hike, and I was relieved to have passed the test. After returning to the trail twenty-five pounds lighter, armed with a new inhaler, and carrying lighter gear, I cannot recall a more satisfying hike than Mount Princeton or a happier drive home from a trailhead with Emme.

About two weeks after Mount Princeton, before we could even plan an encore and research the next fourteener to take on, Emme and I found ourselves on the trail of a mountain we hadn't even planned on climbing that day. And it was not just any mountain—it was Mount Elbert, which, at 14,440 feet, is the highest point in Colorado. It was possibly even higher than the 300-section at Coors Field. But in this case, the height had little to do with the difficulty of the hike. A nine-mile round trip, Mount Elbert was known to be among the easiest of the fifty-eight fourteeners. While it is every bit as much vertical rise as most fourteeners, it is a good path, no challenging pitches, well-marked, and rated Class 1 all the way up. It is a popular choice as a person's first—and often only—career fourteener.

Emme and I wound up on Mount Elbert Trail only because we had been looking for a change of scenery after having worn out the many trails above Independence Pass. Choosing a dirt road in Twin Lake, we then came upon a sign for the Mount Elbert trailhead and decided to take it. From what I had read about Mount Elbert, the early part of the trail would be clean and the incline modest, perfect for a low-key, two-mile nature walk before we turned around.

After a couple of miles, however, I could tell that Emme was firing on all cylinders and in full hiking mode, and I didn't want to be the one to tell her we were about to turn around. Just getting started myself, I was breathing smoothly and, moreover, it was a gorgeous day. Should we keep on going? A resounding "yes"—if it were possible. The next question was whether we had supplies, and the answer was that I always carry a full day pack stocked with water and energy bars, although on this day I hadn't packed sandwiches. Even after the trail began making significant elevation gains, my exertion level felt more than manageable as we reached the tree line and then beyond. The next thing we knew, the summit was in sight, maybe 1,000 feet up. No reason to stop now.

When we reached the summit, there was a pile of rocks resembling a mini-fortress that had likely been built to shield people from heavy winds. Emme immediately sought out and climbed onto the highest boulder and stared straight ahead, as she always did. As she gazed out at the mountains, I watched her and wondered what she thought about on these summits. Only the sounds of the rushing wind could interrupt our thoughts; there wasn't another person on the summit. Neither of us was complaining.

Since we didn't have real food, I limited our stopover at the summit to a hard five minutes, after which we began our descent to the car. After four and a half downhill miles and a one-hour ride back over the Pass to Aspen, we were home by mid-afternoon. I blame the exuberance of nailing an unplanned fourteener for the normally off-limits blueberry muffin I ordered to go along with my post-hike coffee. For her part, Emme spent a little extra time at the food bowl at home, but that was the only giveaway that she'd just taken a nine-mile hike to the highest point in the state. Maybe I'm biased, but the look on her face seemed to shout, *I love surprises. Let's do more of those.*

Along with a rotating cast of regular hiking partners in Shan, Laura, and Rick Peckham, Emme and I proceeded to climb a total of nine fourteeners over the next thirteen months, our most prolific hiking period to date. There is no doubt that the combination of an inhaler for my lungs and having less of me to carry up the mountains was an important part of the formula that improved my game on high-altitude climbs. The intangible part of the equation was the constant presence of Emme, whose every adventure on a mountain trail was a master class on the joy of having found one's life passion.

Emme's age had become a factor to consider, even though she hadn't lost a step and had maintained ninja-level climbing skills. When we celebrated her tenth birthday with a new orange hiking vest on January 31, 2011, the conventional 7:1 dog years-to-human years ratio put Emme at seventy years old. But at least two authorities—Cesar Milan, the Dog Whisperer, and the American Kennel Club—offer different formulas that make similar assumptions. Cesar and the AKC both factor in dogs' fast maturity in their first two years, with Cesar putting the number at 21 and the AKC at 24. After that, Cesar puts the ratio at 4:1, the AKC at 5:1. At $(Age - 2) \times 4 + 21$, Cesar puts Emme at fifty-three in human years. With $(Age - 2) \times 5 + 24$, the AKC pegs her at sixty-four. The good news was that both calculations kept her younger than me, which seemed about right. She had already regarded herself as the CEO

of our home since a week after her arrival in 2001; I didn't need
our alpha dog holding age seniority over me, as well.

One of the highlights of the nine fourteeners after Mount Princeton took place on Mount Massive, the mountain with the second-
highest elevation in Colorado at 14,421 feet. Stories made the
rounds about a friendly rivalry between fans of Mount Massive and
those who favored the highest peak, Mount Elbert, which Emme
and I had hiked just a month earlier. Before the U.S. Geological
Society reevaluated elevation figures based on more accurate technology, Mount Elbert was measured to be just twelve feet higher
than Mount Massive, resulting in the stacking of boulders thirteen
feet high on Massive's summit by its nearby Leadville devotees,
who then claimed number one status. But the problem was that
the man-made peaks never lasted long enough to be evaluated by
the geologists, as Mount Elbert's fans would then make their way
to the summit of Mount Massive and knock the ad-hoc structure
to the ground. Who knew that fourteeners had their own fan clubs?

As we hiked down Mount Massive, Emme abruptly stopped and
visibly perked up. Within a few seconds I heard the unmistakable
chirp of a marmot, easy to identify but often hard to locate, given the
complicated acoustics of the rocks on the trail. But all you needed
to do was look at Emme. In her best imitation of an English pointer
dog in the freeze position, she was directly facing a rock about thirty
feet off the trail. Perched on top sat an all-white marmot.

We found ourselves face-to-face with the celebrated albino
marmot—star of local media, climbers' blogs, and the UCLA
marmot study. Assisted by Emme's canine superpowers, we had
somehow come upon this rare sighting amidst a sea of rocks and
boulders above the tree line. As much as this might sound like

an exaggeration to nonlocals, a chance encounter with the albino marmot was the Colorado equivalent of stumbling upon Bigfoot. Fortunately, I was able to snap a clear and unambiguous photo of the marmot, unlike the low-res, blurry messes claiming to be Bigfoot that are seen on the front page of supermarket tabloids. I apologize to the Bigfoot believers among our readers, but I remain highly skeptical. As you have gathered by now, I like evidence, and decades of blurry photographs don't cut it for me. By the way, if there is a Bigfoot out there, you'd think that at least once he'd have been spotted by someone with a decent camera.

The rare albino marmot on Mount Massive.

Emme must have known we had come across an exceptional marmot because unlike the dozens of marmots she had kept separated from our hiking sticks or chased back into their holes, she maintained her frozen pose without initiating pursuit. *It smells like a marmot—exactly like a marmot. But it's white. What's up here? Let's continue to observe.*

What I wish I could have explained to her was that the albino marmot isn't an albino at all. The recipient of a rare recessive gene, the animal has a condition called leucism, which is a reduction in pigment observed in any number of squirrel populations, as well as in mammals such as lions, horses, and rock pigeons. Albinism, on the other hand, results from a lack of melanin production. The big differences are the albino animals having pale yellow skin and red eyes, both coming about from reduced melanin, compared to animals affected by leucism, which usually have bright white skin and who have natural eye color. This marmot was a beautiful sight to behold in nature.

Given the events and social obligations scheduled around the Fourth of July in Aspen, the start of the 2011 climbing season was slightly delayed. Emme didn't get to hike her first fourteener as a ten-year-old until after the holiday—but we didn't wait long. I booked us for July 5, with Laura joining us for our climb to the summit of Mount Bierstadt. A great opener for our late start to fourteener season, Bierstadt would be a seven-mile hike with about 2,800 feet of elevation that by this time seemed more like a prep climb, especially compared with the more demanding hikes as the summer unfolded.

After overnighting in Georgetown, we arrived at the trailhead and shoved off at 7 AM to clear skies and, for once, moderate morning temperatures. There were switchbacks for about 500 feet up to 12,300 feet, then a steep and rocky slope that led past 13,000 feet. When Emme sensed that the path to the summit was straightforward from there, she ran out ahead of us and got to the summit first. This was her fourteenth fourteener—say that three times fast—and her first one in the books for 2011.

On the descent, an unusual circumstance occurred—Emme began veering off to one side and deviating from the same path we had ascended just a short while ago. This made no sense to me, as Emme's sense of direction on the way down from mountains was usually right on the notes, compared with the occasional improvisation—generally spot-on, by the way—that she employed on the uphill climbs.

Rather than calling her back this time, I decided to follow where she had gone to see what had drawn her attention. The sight was one I will always remember—about twenty-five feet off the route on a pile of boulders sat an Asian man chanting "Om" (the Hindu mantra pronounced "aum"), staring straight ahead. I saw Emme climb to the top of giant rock slabs that rested on the edge of a precipitous drop-off, which positioned her to the gentleman's left. Like her meditating friend, she also looked out into the distance, cocking her head at the same visual angle assumed by her new friend. By this time, the gentleman had stopped the chanting, as I stood quietly to the side, wondering what would come next. Nothing happened. Both Emme and the gentleman remained completely quiet and motionless. As I drew closer to them, Emme still didn't acknowledge me, so I continued to quietly observe. My impulse was to burst out laughing, but I suppressed it out of respect to the man—and to Emme.

It was only after another five minutes passed that the man broke the silence, looking down at Emme and then toward me. "That dog has a human mind," he said with conviction. "What kind of dog is it?" When I told him that her name is Emme and that she was an Australian terrier, he said he felt her presence the moment she arrived in the area and sat next to him on the rock. He referred to their time together as a tandem meditation. When I asked why he had ceased chanting when Emme arrived, he explained that chanting can sometimes become a distraction in a tandem meditation. All I could do was nod in agreement.

Laura had already quietly approached and heard the tail end of our exchange. We said our goodbyes, and the Asian gentleman then looked directly at Emme and thanked her by name.

Emme's meditation with her new friend reminded me of when she looked to the east from our Zen hangout, the small ledge near the rocky peak up from the Independence Pass parking lot. She would sit still there as well, as we both took in the views. Maybe she had been practicing meditation on our hikes all along.

After a short while on the descent, after acting as though what we had just seen had been no big deal, Laura broke the silence. "If I hadn't seen and heard all that myself, I never would have believed it," she said.

But this is Emme, I thought. *I hear this all the time.*

Missouri Mountain in late August 2011 became the final fourteener of the ten we had completed since being buoyed by the success of the Mount Princeton hike. Missouri was a personal choice of Laura, a Kansas City native and current winter resident, and her friend, Shari Appelbaum. Shari was physically fit and unquestionably braver than the average bear—she was working at that time as a photojournalist assigned to notoriously dangerous assignments such as Yemen, Pakistan, and even North Korea—and that's saying something as a blond, very American-looking woman. I am not much of a talker on hikes, especially when hiking uphill, but listening I can do. Shari was a lively, entertaining, and informative storyteller, and I recall thinking that her exploits would make for a fascinating action film. The chatter between Laura and Shari was like listening to my own personal radio show.

The final hike of the year was an outlier in that it was not a fourteener or even a thirteener. But at 12,953 feet, Mount Sopris has all the fixings of a Class 2 fourteener—elevation gain, round-trip mileage, sketchy rocks, and impressive summit views. Named after Captain Richard Sopris, who had followed the rarely taken career path of full-time prospector to mayor of Denver, Mount Sopris held special meaning for me for another reason: it is one of the most visible mountains in the Aspen-Carbondale corridor, rising 5,500 feet from the valley floor. And by *visible*, I also mean that you can see it from just about every window in our house. This was a mountain that was calling out to me every day to be climbed. It was time.

Turning this excursion into an overnight camping trip had been mostly my doing. As a one-day trip, Mount Sopris would require a 5,000-foot elevation gain as part of the fourteen-mile round trip. Online posts listed the average hiking time as ten hours, to which my "controlled" hiking pace could easily tack on an extra three or four hours. That would not be a fun day for me. Instead, I suggested that we backpack with full overnight gear to Thomas Lakes, a 4.5-mile hike with a 1,580-foot elevation gain, set up camp there, and summit the next morning. I lobbied hard to divide this climb into segments and was glad when I prevailed. My new high-tech gear and lighter pack also gave me confidence there would be no turnaround on this ascent.

The team for this outing would be among the best assembled for a hike that ever included me. Brett and Amos had come to town to close the season, and we would also be joined by Rick and Diana Peckham, enthusiastic participants when we hiked the four peaks in one day for charity back in 2008. Another member of the ensemble was the month of September, which meant the brilliant yellows and oranges from the aspen trees that accompany the change of seasons. Combined with the sunny weather, the blue skies, an exciting mountain, and the prospect of a campout, this was pretty much heaven on earth for me. I was also thankful for a summer of extensive and successful climbing, which added to my confidence and fitness levels on the trip.

With two strong guys along on the hike—don't look at me—we had the required muscle to carry the essentials needed for a blow-out steak dinner. Brett took on the most weight, carrying my tent, two bladders of wine, and part of the haul of food. Rick P. also had an important job, carrying up the steaks, the water filter, and food for the dogs, both of whom were on their first camping trip. Setting off at 1:45 PM, we reached Thomas Lakes at 4:15 PM by way of a coherent trail that presented no real complications. Once at the camping area, we set about cutting firewood, setting up the tents, and stringing lines high across two trees to hang our food at night (protection from bears).

Emme was clearly engaged with the new setting and buzz of activity. She was carefully observing everything and everybody, taking it all in. For her, camping was a new experience, with all tents needing to be fully and repeatedly inspected. Also, her sense of smell was on hyper speed, having recognized back when we loaded the 4Runner that we had brought along more than turkey sandwiches.

As we began cooking over the campfire, I heard Emme's distinctive *rrufff*, which was often her indication that an animal was nearby but not yet visible. Amos must have picked up the scent, as well, because in moments they had gone from high-alert status to racing off into the distance. Moments later, a small group of cows appeared, which meant that our camping area was doubling as the "free range" for a local rancher. As we saw when Emme met the bulls, the U.S. Forest Service allocates grazing rights on government land to ranchers who are committed to raising high-quality local beef. Once the cows looked around, shrugged, and returned to wherever they had been, the dogs settled down.

I can only hope the cows didn't catch wind of the ribeye steaks we had begun cooking over the fire. The rest of the meal—grilled corn, garlic mashed potatoes, and dried kale—should have qualified us for a James Beard Award in the highly competitive "campfire-cooking" category. Paired with two liters of Walter Hansel Pinot Noir and the awe-inspiring outdoor setting at sunset, our dinner that night was absolutely one for the ages.

As temperatures fell further with the onset of darkness, we huddled around the fire, stoking it, and feeding it firewood. Then the dogs began acting up again. Since we were completely in the wild and at an altitude low enough to be surrounded by forest, the dogs could have been reacting to anything from small rodents to coyotes and mountain lions. That we were in the dark and hearing concern from the dogs put us on edge—until we saw about six pairs of enormous white eyes staring at us from the darkness. Within a short time, we were able to identify our visitors as the cows, all black in color except for the whites of their eyes. It was a very cool sight.

With our eye on an early—but not too early—ascent time to the summit, we adjourned to our respective tents at around 9:30 PM. I crawled into mine and called for Emme to join me. Walking in, she proceeded to circle the perimeter of the tent a few times from head-to-toe, just as she did in her home when she was a puppy. It had become much colder once the sun had set, and the next thing I knew, Emme had crawled into my sleeping bag with me. There isn't enough room in sleeping bags for an extra being, so I left it partially unzipped so she could fit. We wound up depending on each other's body heat rather than a zipped-closed sleeping bag for warmth that night. Maybe Emme the Aussie terrier had intuitively known about the old Australian expression "three-dog night," based on how many dogs someone would need to have in close quarters in order to stay warm when sleeping outdoors on a cold night. After an enjoyable climb and a fantastic meal at the Thomas Lakes campgrounds, it would go down as a one-dog night for Emme and me.

The camping area we chose placed us in an ideal location from which to start the next day's climb. This meant there was no reason to enforce the start-in-the-dark kickoff times that had become routine on past hikes to handicap for my "speed" and to avoid thunderstorms. Still, our group was on the trail by first light at 7 AM, which set us off on a path around the lakes. It wasn't long, however, before a steep uphill on the left took us to a ridge where things became rocky. The quirk of Mount Sopris is the two false summits we needed to get past, the second of which was craggy and steep. Once on final approach, we came face-to-face with Capitol Peak, the king of all Colorado fourteeners and the mountain that stood over us during the walk with Bev on Capitol Lake Trail. But seeing it this close and so clear confirmed there was no reason to even consider it anytime soon. As I focused intensely on Capitol Peak, the more I couldn't imagine how I would climb it and the more I understood how it has killed so many climbers.

After lingering long and eating our sandwiches at the summit, we reluctantly loaded up and began to head down. At first, the hiking presented no problems, but as we got back to the second false summit (first one on descent), we came upon the bigger, sharper, and steeper rocks that gave us pause on the way up. But Brett was the first to notice that the dogs were having increasing trouble dealing with the rocks on the way down, and he didn't want to risk their legs getting jammed or shredded in the cracks.

The next thing I saw was Brett loading all fifty-five pounds of Amos over his shoulders, wrapping around the back of his neck and on top of his pack. Watching him pick his way down those sharp, teetering rocks while so top-heavy was an impressive display of strength and balance.

Brett carrying fifty-five pounds of Amos and a twenty-five-pound pack on a difficult and unsteady rocky decline.

Rick Peckham lifting Emme down those same rocks to avert the chance of leg damage. This was the first lift for Emme on any mountain. The Sopris summit is on the upper left.

Rick P. then decided to give Emme a ride, marking the first time in hiking seventeen tall mountains that she had ever been picked up. Rick made the perfect call in this instance, however. His instincts on the hiking trail were as good as it got.

The good news for Brett and Rick was that the patch of rocks soon disappeared, allowing the dogs to resume the hike under their own power. Making good time, we reached the camp by 1:30 PM, packed up the tents and gear, and reached the car from the camp in a little under ninety minutes.

It had been a glorious two days of hiking, communing with nature and spending time with three of my favorite people and

Brett, Emme, and me back at the car after a long but exhilarating day on a majestic mountain.

our wonderful dogs. For the record books, Emme's achievement of never having been picked up on a fourteener—or thirteener—had remained intact, given that Mount Sopris came in at just under 13,000 feet. The mountain that beckons to me through our windows every day had been a fitting way to cap off what turned out to be an ambitious fifteen-month schedule in the mountains—eleven fourteeners, plus all the challenges one could ask for with Mount Sopris. No matter how you calculated human years to dog years, Emme and I were now two hikers of a "certain age," yet we had just closed the book on our most exciting hiking season to date. And for that I had every reason to be grateful.

The takeaway from the 2011 season was initially all about the numbers—six incredible hikes in a little over three months, the eleven trouble-free fourteeners that followed turning around on Snowmass, and sixteen summits of 14,000 mountains that Emme reached in her career. Both Emme and I had been at the top of our games from June 2010 through the end of the 2011 season when we descended Mount Sopris. The temptation was to push things with a similarly aggressive schedule for dog-friendly four-teeners in 2012, to climb as many mountains as we could while the fourteener window was still open for us. But as winter turned to spring and as the summer season drew closer, my goals and perspective began to shift. What remained with me from last year was less about the number of mountains and more about the special moments while on those climbs—Emme meditating with her new friend, steaks around the campfire with good friends, Shari's mountain lecture about Yemen, and Brett carrying Amos over the sharp rocks. I was thankful for the healthy reboot that made all these new experiences possible when it looked like I might need to scale back on high-altitude climbing.

As I approached the age of sixty-nine and with Emme in her twelfth year, the number of our hikes would be determined by whether we were still able to navigate the big mountains. We would take nothing for granted, and we would remember to celebrate the glory of each hike—the early mornings on the trailhead, the gor-geous wildflowers on the trail, and the rock climbs to the summit —and the turkey-and-Swiss sandwiches once we arrived there.

In the spring of 2012, our plans to explore the mountains together during that summer—or any summer—were perma-nently shattered. While hiking on our favorite trail at the top of

Independence Pass, Emme began behaving peculiarly. Spotting a couple ahead of us, she proceeded to hike up to them, as she had gone ahead to investigate people so many times on the trail. But as they resumed their ascent, Emme didn't immediately return. And when I called out to her, she didn't respond, leading me to believe at first she couldn't hear me. Instead, she kept following the couple and never turned around, which was also highly irregular behavior for her. Luckily, the man and woman detected the urgency in my voice, and they were kind enough to turn around, which caused Emme to do the same and eventually come back to me. I didn't know what to make of what I had just seen, but I made the difficult decision right then that until her problems were addressed, there would be no open-space hikes. I simply didn't have the foot speed to catch her if she wandered off like that again, and I couldn't bring myself to put Emme on a leash for our climbs.

Following this incident, Pamela and I noticed more irregular behavior from Emme at home, although it seemed in the early days to stem from hearing loss. But she passed the BAER hearing test, the gold standard of canine hearing tests, and she aced the eyesight test, even though she displayed occasional symptoms of sight loss while walking around the house. Something else had to be affecting her health and behavior to this extent.

Eventually, there came new and observable problems with the way she carried herself, such as bumping into walls, walking in circles, and appearing generally confused. Then things advanced to where she got tangled under a chair and then got lost in our fenced-in backyard. Pamela had been doing research since the hike where Emme first showed symptoms and, after consulting with our veterinarian, to her it became sadly clear that Emme was suffering an all-too-common disease that is often not diagnosed until late stages. Emme had doggie dementia or, as it is more formally called, canine cognitive dysfunction (CCD). There is no single test for the disease, but veterinarians eventually make the diagnosis based on tests they perform to eliminate other explanations for a dog's change in behavior. It is as sad in a dog companion as dementia is with a human, and there is no known way to reverse it.

In a perfect world, Emme and I would have continued to be training partners as we both got older, hiking the local river trails, hills, and local ski mountains. We would climb mountains as far as our bodies would take us, savor every moment, and go home happy from each hike—with Emme perched on the console of the 4Runner. But too often, real life gets in the way of happy endings.

Increasingly, Pamela found herself devoting more time to Emme, not because she needed medical care but because Emme needed to be closely monitored the way a mother must hover over a baby who is learning to walk and prone to find trouble around the house. Pamela also had to carefully supervise mealtime because Emme would finish her bowl and then circle back and eat another dog's meal, seemingly having forgotten that she had just eaten.

Throughout the progression of this insidious disease, Emme remained strong and muscular, having the run of our very large fenced-in yard and often venturing into the pond where she sought out the rocky areas, which I hope brought back fragments of happy and familiar memories of hiking. Wanting to take her on one final visit to the mountains while she was healthy enough to do so, we decided to head up the road to Independence Pass in June 2013. The trail of our usual Zen hike with the tiny, hidden ledge was too steep and difficult to keep her from wandering off, so we chose an alternate called Pt. 13,050. There are any number of summits with no official names that are simply referred to as "Point," followed by their elevation. We had planned to hike the first mile or two, which I knew meant a very manageable and moderate incline for everybody. Pamela accompanied me on this hike, and Emme was joined by our male Aussies, Ralfie and Rocky. I didn't realize how emotional the day would be for me, nor could I foresee how it would all unfold for Emme—back at her home away from home on a mountain trail.

The first half-mile of the hike led us on a path of hard-packed snow that offered isolated areas of soft snow. No problems yet. But then we reached a large section of deeper and softer snow that I didn't think would support Emme's weight. If she sank into the snow, it would require post-holing (leg submerged, then having to pull it all the way out on each stride) to cross the field. This would require significant strength and stamina, and I wasn't sure if Emme could handle it that day. So, much to Emme's protestations, I lifted her up and carried her across the snowfield, post-holing myself into snow that was up to two feet deep, quite a slog.

As I was about to put her down, she began to growl at the two males, who had crossed the field under their own steam. Snarling all the way, she then jumped out of my arms and onto Ralfie for a quick roll in the snow that was over as quickly as it had begun. Believing the fracas had run its course, Pamela and I resumed hiking.

But when I turned about to make sure she was following us, she wasn't there. It was at that moment that I observed a sight most extraordinary—it was Emme retracing my steps back across the

As I let her down, Emme showed her anger at being carried over the snowfield; she was growling and coaxing Ralfie into a fight to show who was boss.

After post-holing back over the snowfield, Emme returns and deliberately shows us she can do it on her own.

snowfield to the *exact* spot where I had picked her up. She then proceeded to do an about-face and walk right back, sinking only a few inches into the snow with each stride but maintaining a glare at me the entire time. I knew what she was saying: *Don't ever lift me. Are we clear? You never did, and I don't need it now.*

When she reached where we were standing, she marched past me as though I didn't exist to reclaim her old position as leader of the hike. As she proudly strutted out ahead of us, I laughed through my tears at this amazing dog. Emme had somehow found a way to outsmart whatever was happening in her brain. If only for a minute or two, she gave us a glimpse of the old Emme, showing off for the crowd and doing things uniquely her way.

Emme's final years were spent dealing with the challenges and indignities of dementia. It pained me to witness her struggle as I carried in my heart so many rich memories of the larger-than-life Aussie terrier who had first led me up hills, then onto the trails of the tallest mountains, and finally, into a new passion in life. As much as I enjoyed every remarkable moment with Emme on the highest mountains, I will cherish even more the simple walks with her down the driveway or to the start of Sunnyside Trail. It didn't matter that on many of those days she didn't always know where she was. Emme remained, now and forever, my hiking partner, and it was important to reassure her that everything would be okay.

As Emme turned fourteen, the dementia steadily worsened, and her hikes became reduced to shorter walks outside the house, as she alternated between confusion and what could optimistically be interpreted as moments of brief recognition. It is too difficult to go into detail, but as every dog owner knows, there comes a time when it is over. That time for Emme was August 27, 2015.

Emme leads the two younger, strong males, Ralfie and Rocky, across the next snowfield. They had to run to catch up. It was a glimpse of the former Emme.

Emme's last look at the high mountains. That is Mountain Boy in the distance, the very mountain that was our first summit years ago. I wonder if she knows it. I think she does.

CHAPTER 13

EVERYBODY'S GOT A MOUNTAIN TO CLIMB

Often when you think you're at the end of something,
you're at the beginning of something else.

—Fred Rogers

Lucky Lady Emme, always in command.

As I had envisioned Emme's golden years unfolding, she would have continued in a new capacity as my coach and full-time training partner. With the same enthusiasm we brought to Mount Princeton, the four peaks, and all our fourteeners together, I saw us hiking the local ski mountains to prepare for my summer climbing seasons in the high mountains. Our time together ended too soon.

When it first became clear that Emme's hiking days were over, my first thought was to weigh the prospect of continuing to climb mountains without her. Nearly all my fourteeners up to that point had been summits I had reached with Emme testing the rocks and leading the way, and I knew that future hikes just wouldn't be the same without her. Over the course of countless trails and sixteen climbs to 14,000-foot peaks, we had forged a deep, unspoken, and almost mystical partnership that made our time on the mountains among the happiest days of my life. I would always miss the joy and enthusiasm she brought to each day and the feats of canine ballet she performed on the high rocks. There is much to say for a good soul whose face and voice and body language conveyed a steady and constant message: *The answer is yes. Of course. Ready? I'm ready now. I'll go wherever you're taking me.*

Given the weather systems in the high altitudes, thunderstorms were regularly in play. At the crack of thunder, Emme would look up with disdain and bark back at the thunder, as if chastising whoever was in charge for being so noisy and possibly cutting short our day on the mountain. As she dealt with snow and hail, the most

I ever heard from her in a hailstorm was an occasional sharp growl when a large chunk of ice hit her where she could feel it. Closer to "Ouch" than a yelp. Something like—*Try that one more time, and I'll really get mad.* Emme was always in control—always protective of me—and even Mother Nature had nothing on her.

There is a special kind of joy, surprise, and amazement that comes from establishing a deep connection and communication with a living being that is not human. A common fallacy is that we are superior as humans, and no animal could possibly have our level of feelings, intelligence, and ability to problem solve. The thrill and surprise come when we realize we could be wrong.

There have been many times when Emme was acutely aware of our situation, knew what needed to be done, where to go, or how to avoid danger. There were so many other times when I needed to communicate with her, and without a doubt, she understood. In fact, we understood each other on a level that, even with my extensive background with animal contact on land and in the sea, I found surprising. That relationship has been a true gift in my life. If one ever is seeking compelling evidence that animal life forms of all kinds evolved from a common core, experiencing a relationship with an animal fulfills that purpose.

We buried Emme in a grave dug through rocks on Red Mountain on the upper edge of our property line. In these mountains, the rocks are made of what is called "mudstone," which is mud hardened into rock. Then with freeze and thaw cycles they cleave and crack. One digs through these rocks and the surrounding dirt by prying them apart and lifting them out. The grave is within twenty feet of Sunnyside Trail, a popular route Emme and I hiked hundreds of times in the six years we lived in that house prior to her decline. A red slab we found on the trail stands with her name and a paw print painted in black. In front of it lies a flat stone we purchased, engraved with the words "Until We Meet Again, Find Peace in Heaven's Hands," surrounded by three perfect heart-shaped stones we found on our fourteener climbs. Fittingly, she is buried next to her longtime sidekick, our beloved Alfie, a grand champion whose passion was dog shows and who won Best in Breed at Westminster in 2007 as a two-year-old.

As many of us feel after losing a dog we love, our hearts were broken when Emme passed away. When she pops into my head, it isn't simply as a flawless mountain climber but also as the puppy who appointed herself as the VP of Security within days of becoming part of our family. To her hiking partner, Emme's life seemed to pass in the blink of an eye. But to a dog, whose concept of time bears no resemblance to ours, maybe it was all good. When I stopped counting the years from her birth and began instead to add up our time on the mountains—and in the car driving to them—the numbers made me smile. Maybe in her mind we had spent several lifetimes together.

Before Emme first grabbed me by the pants leg and then by the heart, I was at a crucial juncture of my life—the intersection of "What's next?" and "Am I too old?" I increasingly searched for what would motivate, sustain, and inspire me for the final third of my life. I have come away with an overriding conviction from these experiences in the mountains with a dog and great friends. Finding and pursuing a passion—any passion—is as important in achieving quality of life in later years as it is at all stages of one's life. A newfound passion for me took the form of mountain climbing. But the point of this book is to inspire readers to find passion anywhere and in anything that stirs the emotions.

The idea of continuing to climb, even more difficult mountains, bounced between my head and my heart; between logic and emotion and between rationality and intuition. I have always thrived on the challenges of business—whether it was starting and running a computer company, advising venture firms, or helping to implement corporate strategies as a board member. For me, genuine excitement about the things I do has always been at my core. Other people might throw around daily bromides like "Another day, another dollar" and "Same old same old," but not me. So, I must admit that I felt like a fish out of water in my earliest days in Colorado—aging out of tech, watching my portfolio crater, and lacking a new adventure to call me out of bed in the morning.

Sometimes, the most profound conclusions are the most obvious, hiding just behind the clutter and noise of daily life. By the time I was considering if mountain climbing could become my next passion, it had already taken hold. I knew this because when suddenly facing the intense year-round fitness program and substantial weight loss it would take to keep Emme and me on the high mountains, there was never a question of turning back—I was all in. Soon, I realized I was no longer accompanying my dog on hikes but had already followed her to the place where she had been leading me all along. As Henry David Thoreau wrote, "I took a walk in the woods and came out taller than the trees."

To me, a summit has come to represent achievement, beauty, and freedom from all man-made artifacts, as well as a defiance of my age. Getting to a summit with my dog Emme has been a communion between us. Without a doubt, she knew when she was at a summit, and I could see that our experience was a shared one. A different look came about her, she was excited, but entranced with the views—same as me. She had the widest "Aussie smile" on her face—same as me, except for the Aussie part. Maybe it was because she knew that once on the summit, it was all downhill from there. If so, that is where we differed, for descending a fourteener is generally a challenge for the human body, with trickier footing than the ascent. Emme never once had problems with footwork in any of our hikes together.

An important part of finding passions throughout one's life is being open to the unconventional places where they might be hiding. Like alpine buttercups, answers can be hiding in the snow, between boulders, or between sharp rocks. They also might even be presented to you in the form of the fearless and uncomplicated example of your dog. Few if any websites or self-help books about late-career lifestyle choices recommend looking to an Australian terrier for vocational guidance. My new road on my life's journey didn't become clear until I expanded the definition of what the road could be, where it could be found, and who would bear the clues about what it looked like. Not in a million years did I expect the road to lead 14,000 feet in the air and that I would find myself on Class 3 and 4 technical climbs in the Rocky Mountains in my early seventies.

People often ask me if I wish I had started climbing mountains as a younger man. The answer is yes, and I have occasionally imagined what it might have been like to climb while in my twenties and thirties. But the upside of having followed Emme into mountain climbing was that it provided me with a late-career passion at the precise time when many people can use a spark. It certainly came at the right time for me. It also helps to find a companion for the road who likes being there as much as you do.

In the end, it was an easy decision for me to continue hiking on the high mountains. I count myself beyond fortunate that Emme led me to a life passion that continues to engage my mind and challenge my body today. Since Snowmass, I haven't turned back yet. When the hikes with Emme ended, I sought out the help of friends and master climbers in taking on Class 3 and 4 climbs I had postponed because they were unsafe for dogs and possibly beyond my abilities. My hope is to continue hiking for as long as my legs, heart, and lungs continue to propel me along. Knowing that climbing 14,000-foot peaks is a finite passion, I cherish each moment, take time to smell both the wine and the roses, and pay careful attention to what the mountains can teach me each day.

Years of winter hikes on Sunnyside Trail played out in a familiar fashion. I would wear snowshoes in order to pack down the trail for the dogs who came out of the house to follow along. But instead of following and taking advantage of the packed snow, Emme invariably took the lead. While it made for a more difficult hike for her, she always loved to make the first tracks, even when this meant plowing through twelve or fourteen inches of new snow. (Her shoulders measured eleven inches high.) The visual from behind was almost comical—that of a black-and-tan dog playing the role of a hopping bunny—disappearing, only to explode out of the snow a second or two later.

After a fresh snow this past winter, I strapped on my boots and snowshoes and set off for a mind-clearing exercise hike up Sunnyside Trail. And not for the first time when I have become lost in my thoughts, I had the feeling I wasn't alone out there on the trail.

It was a time for me to reflect on what Emme had done in her life and what she meant to me. Emme was a dog who never quit in heat, rain, wind, snow, thunder, or when there were endless rocks underfoot. With pure happiness in her heart, she lived for these climbs—even when it meant confronting foxes, countless bigger dogs, a pair of obstinate bulls, and an occasional black bear. Emme had no idea she was a small dog, and she constantly astounded other climbers who couldn't believe she had climbed sixteen fourteeners with no assistance. Above all, she gave herself the assignment of watching out for me in the wild, and it was a mission she took seriously.

On the Sunnyside Trail, I often look up and swear there is an overjoyed Aussie terrier up ahead of me, jumping in and out of the snow to show me the way, just as she always had.

Lucky Lady Emme—a dog with a purpose, a sense of joy, and always in command.

And truly my best friend.

ABOUT THE AUTHORS

Rick Crandall was founder and CEO of the international technology company Comshare, Inc. Currently, he is Chairman of the Board of Donnelley Financial Solutions, as well as serving as Executive Chairman of Pelstar, LLC, a company that was cited for "Private Company Board of the Year" for 2016. He also serves on the boards of five other companies. Rick was named "One of the Five Leading Pioneers of the Computer Industry" and has received Outstanding Entrepreneur awards from both the University of Michigan, his alma mater, and Harvard Business School. A native of New York, Crandall now lives in Aspen, Colorado.

Visit *www.RickCrandallBooks.com* for more information. Here, you will find additional material about the book, plus his blog "On Hiking." It offers a range of advice about the activity for those seeking healthy outdoor fun and exercise—especially when hiking with a dog.

Joseph Cosgriff is a writer and speaker who lives in New York City. He is the co-author (with jazz guitarist/vocalist John Pizzarelli) of *World on a String: A Musical Memoir,* a finalist for Audiobook of the Year in 2014. He also collaborated with clothier Richard Press on *Rebel Without a Suit: The Not-So-Casual Road to Casual Friday.* Cosgriff is also a songwriter whose music was used as the theme of New Jersey Public Radio for six years and whose songs are played on jazz stations and occasionally featured in live performances by discerning musicians.